THE
CREATIVE
PRIORITY

THE CREATIVE PRIORITY

DRIVING

INNOVATIVE BUSINESS

IN THE

REAL WORLD

JERRY HIRSHBERG

HarperBusiness
A Division of HarperCollins*Publishers*

TO LINDA

The Book
Before the Book
Ever After the Book

HarperCollins books may be purchased for educational, business, or sales promotional use. For information please write: Special Markets Department, HarperCollins Publishers, Inc., 10 East 53rd Street, New York, NY 10022.

FIRST EDITION

Designed by Elina D. Nudelman

Library of Congress Cataloging-in-Publication Data

Hirshberg, Jerry, 1939–
The creative priority : driving innovative business in the real world /
by Jerry Hirshberg. — 1st ed.
p. cm.
Includes bibliographical references and index.
ISBN 0-88730-830-9
1. Product management. 2. Marketing—Management.
3. Creative ability in business. 4. Automobile industry and trade.
I. Title.
HF5415.15.H55 1998
658.5—dc21 97-2895

98 99 00 01 02 ❖/RRD 10 9 8 7 6 5 4 3 2 1

We shall not cease from exploration
And the end of all our exploring
Will be to arrive where we started
And know the place for the first time.

T. S. Eliot[1]

Contents

Contents

Acknowledgments

The dubious notion of trying to write a book while running a business—which quickly turned into trying to run a business while writing a book—was not my own. Rather, it was suggested and encouraged by a small army: a dear friend, an astute reader, a creativity-enabler par excellence, a clinical and organizational psychologist, a mother, and a wife, all of whom are Dr. Linda Hirshberg. Infinite love and gratitude.

Critical to the business of making the book a reality were several strong and remarkable persons: Sandra Dijkstra, literary agent, who knew just which thread to pull to unravel a tangled mass of ideas; Adrian Zackheim, publisher of HarperCollins Business division, who helped me find and recognize my own voice; Suzanne Oaks, editor, for her guidance and enthusiasm during the initial stages; Laureen Rowland, editor, whose sensitive readings and spot-on suggestions sharpened and clarified the book's focus.

Acknowledgment is also due Roy Carlisle, literary agent, and John Archer, writer, for their early support and recognition of the value of these ideas on creativity in business.

Gratitude, of course, to Nissan and its executives, for fostering, accommodating, and protecting its far-flung satellite and for using the fruits of its labors. And to my co-travelers and co-discoverers at

Nissan Design International, who have brought the principles of the *creative priority* to life.

A small but vital percentage of our staff are Japanese dispatches. Over the years we have been favored with some outstanding individuals who were significant contributors, intercultural bridges, and real members of the family. They are too numerous to mention, but I must single out Kazumi Yotsumoto, Hidehiro Iizuka, Kengo Ishida, Hiroshi Matsubara, and Haruo Kamata for their sensitive participation in the adventure, and their friendship.

Also too numerous to mention by name are all those I used as sounding boards, but I must acknowledge Tom Semple, Bruce Campbell, Sheldon Payne, Nick Backlund, Allan Flowers, and Lou Knierim. Thanks are due each of them for their invaluable input. Most especially to Dr. Stan Fevens for his ever-valuable reflections.

One of the very few without whom this book could not have been written is Yvette Prado, executive assistant. Her fine work, character, and capacity to remain my friend through it all have been among the great joys of this project.

I was incredibly fortunate to have at my disposal the talents of four exceptional young people who happen to be my sons and daughters-in-law. Special thanks to Glen, writer and teacher, and Kim, writer and soon-to-be Ph.D. folklorist, for their availability and far-more-critical-than-they-realized insights and writerly wisdom; to Eric, advertising executive and creative director, for his splendid cover design and pivotal observation some years ago that NDI was "probably [my] most significant design"; and to Tara, contemporary art dealer, for her continuing interest and support.

Creative drive grows from diverse soils, and in retrospect, this book, like much of my work, grew from a soil richly nourished by my parents, Ed and Lill Hirshberg. Particular acknowledgment must go to an extraordinary mother, for taking all the scribbles, noises, and notions seriously in the first place.

Introduction:
Unleashing Creativity

Another requirement for the creative person which is even more difficult to accept: gullibility . . . a willingness to explore everything: to be open, innocent and naïve before rejecting anything.

Silvano Arieti[1]

The caller identified himself as Mr. Andy Zaleta of Korn-Ferry, the largest executive headhunting firm in the world. He asked if I'd be interested in establishing and directing an international design facility for one of the world's largest non-American auto manufacturers. Along with continuing to be an active designer, I would help locate the site (anywhere I felt appropriate), find and work with an architect, hire a select staff, and create a unique organization and methodology for designing real cars for the real world.

"Go to hell, Lenny," I said, and hung up.

Len Casillo was then chief designer for Oldsmobile at the General Motors Technical Center in Warren, Michigan, while I held the equivalent position for Buick. He was not to be trusted. It was 1979, a time of increasing stagnation in Detroit, and pranks provided an outlet and a measure of sanity for the creative staff. The job description promised a once-in-a-lifetime opportunity to establish a potentially ideal creative environment, and many locations in America seem inviting when you are in the throes of a Midwestern winter.

Mr. Zaleta called back. "Mr. Hirshberg," he said, chuckling, "I don't know who Lenny is, but this is not a game show. This could happen to you."

***

The company turned out to be Nissan Motor Corporation. They had been making cars since 1914, and had been exporting their product to the United States under the name of Datsun since 1958. They have had an established corporate presence here since 1960. By 1980, fifty percent of their products were exported, including 574,000 vehicles to the United States alone.

Around that time, Mr. Takashi Ishihara, then president of Nissan, decided to bring the intuition of Western designers into contact with the technological agility of Japan. He correctly perceived design as a form of nonverbal communication and realized he was speaking a foreign visual tongue to more than half his market. He further realized that, whereas Japan had already reached exalted levels of technological sophistication, it had not yet achieved equivalent levels of design excellence. In order to elevate the design level of its products and break free of its conservative, "local" taste, Nissan conceived the solution: to start a creative satellite that would be liberated from Nissan's internal politics and provide it with the authority to operate independently. After Italy, England, France, and Germany were considered—each a country with a rich history of automobile design—America was selected as the location for the facility. It would become known as Nissan Design International (NDI). Now he needed someone to help create and direct it.

***

Leaving an excellent position with the world's largest, most successful manufacturing company was not a matter to be taken lightly. In fact, I was six months along in the interview process before I began to comprehend the global shift my life was to take. By this time, Korn-Ferry was out of the picture and it was apparent that I was one of a few remaining candidates. I was in a suite in what was then called the Renaissance Center Hotel in Detroit for a face-to-face interview with Mr. Kazumi Yotsumoto. He had been the key executive entrusted to select an individual to help him bring NDI into being. Later he became its first president. A slight man, Mr. Yotsumoto was nevertheless an imposing presence. He wasted neither words nor gestures. I could feel him reading me, sizing me up, yet I rarely caught his eye (not the last time I was to experience this phenomenon with Japanese colleagues). There was a focused, intense quality to him; his precise tie perfectly bisected the angle between his starched collars. On my first trans-Pacific flight I remember crawling up from a fitful airline sleep, oily and cramped, to find him sound asleep next to me, his seat in the fully upright position; he was powder-dry, wrinkle-free, his suit was buttoned, his tie up. Educated as an architect, he was one of three distinguished individuals selected by Japan after the war to come to America to learn all he could about design.

No formal interpreter now assisted the interviewing process, which meant we had a limited vocabulary with which to work. There were questions about my management style and design philosophy, as well as reflections on my years with General Motors; but the most important communication occurred nonverbally. Without a common language, Mr. Yotsumoto and I were groping for connections from utterly alien starting points. We both knew that what we were embarking on had never really been done before, so there were no evident right or wrong answers. From the outset, I'd decided to be myself rather than play a part I felt the Japanese might think acceptable. On the other hand, I was willing to fully immerse myself in the multiple layers and alien cadences of the bicultural communication process, and leave value judgments behind as much as possible. Our questions for each other were basic, forcing us to deal with fundamentals and assumptions not generally addressed among colleagues within a common culture. There were often long pauses between question and response, and sometimes extended periods of stillness. My instinct at first was to fill all the awkward voids and make everything comfortable, but that felt inappropriate now. When referring back to a particularly quiet and "uneventful" meeting we'd previously had, he expressed his appreciation simply for the time we'd spent together. And so I found myself relaxing into the silent spaces, realizing they were anything but empty, and sensed a growing fluency in our communication. Much of what seemed most valuable was emerging from the rhythms, body language, context, and moods of the interaction, yielding volumes about my understanding of this complex Japanese man and, unexpectedly, about myself.

During this particular interview, as I began to answer a question about my management style, Mr. Yotsumoto suddenly rose from his chair and walked toward me. I stopped speaking midsentence as he approached the sofa on which I sat, and my eyes suddenly became moist. He sat down next to me and said quietly, "Hashibag-san (the closest he could get to the phonetic equivalent of my name in Japanese), let me now tell you about my wife and son."

After the interview, I went home to my wife, Linda, who was understandably eager for a decision after almost a year of negotiations. "Well, are we going to move or aren't we?" she asked. I replied, "Hon, I just got the job."

There had been no slap on the back or "Welcome aboard, kid!" from Mr. Yotsumoto. Just a moment of shared intimacy, a bond of trust, and a spark of connection. Something significant was happening in the void of our mutual foreignness, and while nothing quite like this had happened to me before, it all felt strangely familiar, like the first stroke of paint thrust upon a threateningly blank canvas which felt suddenly alive with possibility.

***

The opportunities and potential of this offer were both intimidating and enticing, as was the promise of leaving a company that had ceased having fun. I had never intended to stay more than a few years at General Motors. I had certainly not intended to stay for sixteen years. My time there, however, provided an invaluable springboard and reference for shaping NDI. It offered an intimate grasp of the workings of the world's mightiest corporation. It also afforded me the frustration of experiencing the decline of its powers, all from the unique and revealing perspective of design. The contrast between the openness and energy I found there in the early sixties and the closed-down rigidity I felt when I left in 1979 made an indelible impression on me.

I had been educated as a general product designer, and worried that limiting myself to one product, the automobile, would be restrictive. There was (and still is) a ludicrous antipathy between automobile and product designers that began at school and continues in the professional world. Automobile designers were seen as shallow stylists who generated cosmetic, flashy trends, while product designers were thought of as dry intellectuals lacking talent, soul, or flair. They hardly seemed members of the same profession, which appeared as misguided to me then as it does now.

As an experiment in 1963, the GM Styling Department had gone outside its traditional source schools, the Art Center of Pasadena and the Center for Creative Studies of Detroit, to seek fresh design talent from such diverse places as Pratt Institute of New York, the Illinois Institute of Technology, the University of Bridgeport, and the Cleveland Institute of Art. These schools offered degrees in the broad field of industrial design but not one in transportation design. Chuck Jordan, then GM's director of design, wanted to hire a few designers with different and possibly broader perspectives to interact with and stimulate the more traditionally educated automobile designers. He realized he might be accepting a few individuals without much gasoline in their veins, but was willing to take that risk.

I knew I'd be working in a place where most of my colleagues would be practicing design as a means of being close to their first love, cars, while I'd be working with cars because of the rich, complex opportunities they represented to the process of design. I was approaching the job from a fresh (and, I would learn, not terribly popular) perspective. But being a "hired renegade" was simply too delicious an opportunity to pass up, and I was impressed by the corporation's expansive posture at the time.

When I first arrived, GM was the supreme icon of power and success for America. And it was the pinnacle for anyone wanting to design cars in this country. There was a spectacular array of talent under the fiery leadership of William Mitchell, the VP of Styling, upon my arrival. Passionate about cars, motorcycles, and racing, his veins were saturated with gasoline. His entire focus at the time was on taming the styling excesses reached in Detroit in the fifties while at the same time setting the pace among the "Big Three." And he was making considerable progress with such exceptional vehicles as the Chevy Corvair, the first Buick Riviera, and the early Corvettes.

I moved into management rather swiftly and had considerable opportunity to experiment with leading the creative process. I was working with stimulating people, such as a rising young engineer named John DeLorean, and was making some impact on such cars as the first Pontiac Firebirds, the Grand Prix, and the GTO.

Mitchell's ability to mobilize an entire department (and most of the corporation) around his cause left a deep impression on me.

Under him, Styling felt itself on a mission. But when he wanted to apply the brakes or change directions, he could be brutally direct. Upon being labeled with one of his colorful but deadly metaphors, a design he wanted to trash died an immediate and eternal death. In response to a car design with a particularly high belt-line (small side-glass relative to door height), he said a passenger in it would feel and look like a "goddamn apple in a bathtub." Confronted by a particularly hefty rear view with bulging fenders extending out beyond the tires, he bellowed that the car looked like "a fat lady on high heels." When faced with having to downsize GM's cars in response to the oil crisis as well as the new, economically scaled competition emerging from Japan, he said it was "like tailoring for dwarves."

He was no less subtle in expressing his feelings about people. When he saw passion and flair in someone, while not exactly becoming a mentor, he was occasionally willing to pass along some of his unique perspective. Shortly after I was promoted to chief designer of an advanced studio, he called me aside for some counsel. As I had been made a manager so soon, I was the youngest person in the studio at the time, and he was concerned about my saying what had to be said. "Kid (he called everyone kid), the secret to great leadership is being able to say 'fuck you' in the morning and 'how 'bout lunch' by noon."

Mitchell had no patience, however, for listening to a designer (or anyone else) explain the theory behind a design, describe its intended customers, or talk about the world in which it would exist. Words were not to be trusted at GM Styling. Lines and forms were. Nevertheless, he could be outrageous and reckless with his own words, even in interviews with the media. He laughed off his own gaffes with a shrug, but was far less generous about public comments from anyone else on his staff, something I learned the hard way.

***

While serving as chief designer of Buick Studio in 1975, I was interviewed by Pat Bedard of *Car & Driver* magazine about the just-released Buick Regal. The car was regarded as relatively "clean" (devoid of excessive fussiness) and understated by then-current standards. While my predecessor, Wayne Kady (who went on to become chief of Cadillac), had at least as much to do with the Regal as I, Bedard liked my words about it and verbally hoisted me up on a charging white stallion, a young knight fighting bravely for simpler, more aesthetically efficient design against Mitchell and a phalanx of aging bosses who still clung to their "padded uppers," "opera windows," and assorted automotive jewelry.

When advance copies of the magazine came out, it caused a considerable stir. Chuck Jordan called me over the weekend and told me there could be serious repercussions. I hadn't seen the article yet and tried in vain to recall every question and answer while I tossed and turned all night Sunday.

Monday morning I received ominous visits by Mitchell's next-in-command, Irv Rybicki, and Irv's next-in-command, Jordan. All was quiet until ten o'clock, when my secretary told me I was to report to Mitchell's office, not noted for its coziness in the best of circumstances. It was roughly the size of half a basketball court and decorated in cruise-ship modern, with a pocket door that electronically whooshed open and whooshed shut behind me. Mitchell's head glowed bright red above his battleship-sized desk.

"Did you say the shit in that article, kid?"

"Well, I . . ." was all I got in.

"Well, you're fucking fired. Get outta here."

I couldn't believe my ears, which were throbbing, and I was in a kind of trance during the long walk back to my office. By the time

I got there, though, I was strangely calm, even relieved. There was a sudden flurry of activity around me. Jordan and Rybicki returned and expressed support, as did George Elges, the general manager of Buick and no great admirer of Mitchell. Calls were being made, some, I later found out, to very high places. Meanwhile, like clockwork, two burly hall guards had arrived and the GM separation mechanism clicked into gear. I was given a cardboard box and told to start packing. The guards were pleasant, but it was clear there would be no deviation from procedure. I had begun to say my good-byes to the stunned staff when my secretary told me to report back to Mitchell's office. It was now approaching noon.

Whoosh. Whoosh. I was back in the helm station, Mitchell's head still looming above his battleship-sized desk, but glowing considerably less red. He rose and came around to the front of the desk, leaned back on it, and crossed his arms. Time stopped.

"Kid, I've been in the same kind of jam you're in. Got a pretty big mouth myself. Those bastards in the press, you just can't trust 'em. Hell, let's go to lunch!"

It was as though someone else had fired me and he was there to commiserate and offer support. I had been fired for roughly two hours and become a member of a small but illustrious elite who'd been cut loose by Bill Mitchell. Now he laid a beefy hand on my shoulder, gave me a smile and a wink, and it was over. From that point on, there was a new level of communication between us. After all, he'd found someone with a similar mouth who had gotten into a situation with the press he was all too familiar with.

And he'd had the opportunity to be the ideal leader; to say "fuck you" in the morning and "how 'bout lunch" by noon.

***

Over time, however, I became increasingly bothered by the closed, static atmosphere at GM and a growing feeling of isolation from the world outside. The emergence of Ralph Nader, consumerism, safety, environmental concerns, and imports all made the sixties and seventies a time of growing turbulence for the automobile industry. But GM continued to display a dangerous reluctance to seriously engage its creative energies and resources in response to these issues. They were seen only as obstacles, not as fresh opportunities for new thinking. What, I wondered, was there to be creative about in the absence of obstacles?

Success is always difficult for a corporation to deal with, and the stratospheric success of General Motors, founded and sustained on the basis of a long sequence of powerful organizational and technological ideas, provided a blinding illusion of security and imperviousness to failure. The corporation was by now five or six generations deep in executives who had never experienced defeat or even the anxieties of second place. The muscles required for creative response to difficult times had atrophied from disuse. General procedures and once-fluid guidelines gradually froze into static codes of thought and behavior in a chilly atmosphere of smug certainty.

GM's resistance to outside change was mirrored by an increasingly stifling corporate culture within, the walls thickening between the departments, each becoming a bastion of protection for well-worn procedures and assumptions buttressed by past successes. As a designer, I felt more and more deprived of all the ferment that occurs across disciplinary boundaries, as well as the dramatic cultural and economic shifts occurring outside the corporate fortress. And the notion of exploring "iffy" paths or taking chances with unfamiliar directions in such an atmosphere was unthinkable.

By the mid-seventies, GM was rapidly becoming the Mantovani of automobile design. Raw yet promising ideas were continually introduced into a formulaic process that inevitably transformed them into visual Muzak. The corporation was living up to its name—a manufacturer of truly general motors.

During my stay there, I learned a great deal about the workings of a corporate supernova and about the power of ideas. My own, in fact, were rewarded with considerable success. At the same time, I was learning how threatening new concepts were to a bureaucracy, and how difficult it was to get them through the system. I felt a sense of remoteness, of being lost in a culture that was becoming increasingly alien to me. The differences in design philosophy and education that had drawn GM and me together in the first place had become barriers, and I felt more and more like a foreigner there, speaking a different language and with a different story in mind. I was ready to move on, when Korn-Ferry called.

***

A few days after I realized I had been selected for the position at Nissan, I was invited to Los Angeles to discuss the actual terms of the relationship: contract, salary, and benefits. Nissan fully understood what I would leave behind at GM after sixteen years of tenure, and wanted to discuss what was necessary to break its famous "golden handcuffs." I felt considerable responsibility for my family, and leaving GM for a position with a foreign company that did not yet have a location, let alone a facility or a name, felt a bit dicey.

In preparation for the negotiations, I met with a friend of Linda's named John O'Meara, one of Michigan's most distinguished labor attorneys. I had read that the Japanese had little experience with formal written agreements, but John suggested I tell them, "Look, you are in Yankee territory now, and we need binding documents to feel secure. So please come halfway, and let's do some form of contract. It would need to be for a brief but reasonable period of time." Armed with Western legal wisdom, I left for my first international negotiation at Nissan's North American sales and marketing headquarters in Carson, California.

At a large conference table surrounded by American and Japanese executives and corporate lawyers, I was asked what my requirements were. "Gentlemen," I responded confidently, "you're in Yankee territory now, and while I'm aware you do not customarily do contracts, I'm going to need one in order to feel a sense of adequate security for my wife and sons." Immediately, Mr. Yotsumoto replied, "For what period of time, Hashibag-san?" Not expecting it to be quite so easy, I managed, "Oh, uh, two or three years will be just fine." At that moment I felt, unaccountably, about ten years old.

Later we took a coffee break from the negotiations, and I asked Mr. Yotsumoto why, after saying I wanted a contract for two or three years, I felt like a child. A smile played around his eyes. "Ah, we expected you to request a contract, but we thought it would be for two to three *generations* of Hashibags!"

I left with a contract, a generous offer, and another glimpse of Japanese character, as well as my own.

❊❊❊

Throughout the flight to California, Linda and I continued to work out all the complex logistics of a cross-country move. Glen and Eric, ages thirteen and eleven, occupied themselves with books, drawings, trading cards, and games, and busied the flight attendants as well with requests for sodas and trips to the cockpit. Just before touchdown in San Diego, Linda turned to me, took my hand, and asked, "Do you by any chance know how to do this?"

"No," I responded, "but finding out is gonna be a lot of fun."

I had already intended to surround myself with a lot of talent—fast! With the kids playing around me, Linda asking tough questions beside me, Detroit diminishing behind me, and the Pacific looming before me, an image was beginning to emerge with utter clarity. This new company would have an organization structured entirely around the needs of the creative process.

After sixteen years of watching fresh ideas struggle against the increasingly unyielding structure of a bureaucratic fortress, this felt like an ideal opportunity to challenge the prevailing paradigm of corporate priorities. Since ideas were going to be essential, why not make creativity the nucleus of this enterprise, and see what kind of atomic and molecular structure might radiate from it.

Of course, from one perspective, it was not such a large leap to have reached this conclusion, given the company president's request to establish a world-class creative facility. However, it is striking how even companies (or departments) capable of innovation rarely extend the principles of the creative process to their organizational management or design. Many of these companies speak with great pride about the way some of their best ideas are generated by renegade bands of "outlaw" talent formed to "buck the system," without considering the possibility of removing the need for outlaws by eliminating creative prohibition in the first place!

GM's design staff sat precariously and uneasily within the corporation's orderly, bureaucratic bounds. While the creative process is essential to the health and success of any corporation, it is rare to find a company both willing and agile enough to adapt to its seemingly odd and unpredictable rhythms.

In establishing a remote satellite separated from the control of headquarters by vast distances, distinct languages, and utterly different cultures, Nissan, a company then dominated by an engineering mentality, was courageously exposing itself to considerable discomfort. But it had a great advantage over GM. Nissan knew what it didn't know, and it was not too proud to learn.

"If you are able to produce consistently professional-level, even exceptional designs that everyone likes, that won't be nearly enough," challenged Ishihara. "You are being created to rock the boat, to shift its design course, and you will not be loved by all."

Since we were independently incorporated, we would have to negotiate the terms of each project. At the same time, we were wholly subsidized by the parent company, so we became outside-insiders, and could simultaneously enjoy the leverage of consultants along with the long-range, in-depth impact of a fully integrated department.

We were contracted at first to design two, and eventually three cars a year. These would take the form of full-sized clay prototypes and a complete set of engineering drawings and accurate specifications. Each project required numerous trips between San Diego and Nissan's design center in Atsugi, Japan. Communications were by any and every available means, which grew to include teleconferencing, satellite transmissions, enhanced fax methodology, and internetting. Between 4:30 and 5:30 P.M. every afternoon in California, the phones lit up and the fax machines stuttered to life as the sun was rising the following morning in Japan. But the real challenges in communications were never technological in nature.

Nissan at first wanted all our concepts to compete with ones from its design center. Although we were apprehensive about the potentially alienating effects of there having to be winners and losers, it was felt that this kind of interaction would best stimulate the Japanese design staff. And while they did not say so, the competition surely provided the parent company a measure of security, just in case NDI did not perform up to expectations.

Over time, however, we noted that the NDI designers were competing with two or even three concepts from Japan against our one. Even though we seldom lost, I later confronted Mr. Jiro Tanaka, a top executive who had a keen grasp of the potential of our enterprise, as to why this was being done. He shot me a knowing, amused glance. "To make it even," he replied, smiling, understanding full well the advantages we increasingly enjoyed.

There would be no pat managerial formulae that could simply be applied. We would fashion an environment focused specifically on what was to be the principal end product of NDI—ideas. And these ideas would not be restricted to cars. Since we were independently incorporated, I sought Nissan's approval to do independent design work for a wide variety of nonautomotive manufacturers. This highly unusual practice (among car design groups) would place our automotive work in the broadest possible context and provide exposure to diverse perspectives and technologies. There would be little that might be thought predictable or expected— except (we hoped) the unexpected.

Given a blank sheet of paper, and unleashed from the traditions and expectations of a single culture, we could now freely envision a fully collaborative environment, where the boundaries between engineering, marketing, sales, planning, and design would be blurred, and where the natural friction between multiple disciplines as well as that between two utterly different cultures might become sources of energy and ferment. While I could not yet imagine the potentially revolutionary implications of organizing a business around the priorities of the creative process, I thought it might be possible to invent, in the chasm between two alien cultures, a new one in which I felt less foreign than I had begun to in my own.

Every aspect of the new facility, from its location to the choice of people to the development of new models of leadership, would be done in concert with an emerging vision of an ideal atmosphere in which ideas might flow, an atmosphere safe for risk and conducive to creative play.

Playing around with things and ideas is vital to innovative thinking, something we all do naturally as kids. But as we grow up, we're taught to be more serious about the ways we think. The guiding image of the facility I carried around with me (and still do) was that of a sandbox. The desired atmosphere: recess.

***

Business begins with an idea. And as never before, its growth, stability, and ultimate success depend upon innovation and a continuing flow of imaginative thought. Throughout this book I will maintain that the most urgent business of business is ideas.

Yet, in many ways, business has never been less well suited to accommodating, let alone stimulating, original thought. Current organizational models revolving around productivity and efficiency at any cost produce a corporate culture hardly conducive to thinking—much less innovative thinking.

 No one in a corporation deliberately sets out to stifle creative thought. Yet, a traditional bureaucratic structure, with its need for predictability, linear logic, conformance to accepted norms, and the dictates of the most recent "long-range" vision statement, is a nearly perfect idea-killing machine. People in groups regress toward the security of the familiar and the well regulated. Even creative people do it. It's easier. It avoids the anxiety of ambiguity, the fear of unpredictability, the threat of the unfamiliar, and the messiness of intuition and human emotion.

A creative bureaucracy is a nearly inconceivable construct. The words simply don't cohere, seeming to cancel each other out. One connotes transparency and agility, the other opacity and turgidity. Is it possible to imagine creative thought thriving in a bureaucracy, or a bureaucracy welcoming creative thought? What fundamental shifts would have to occur to make it so? These questions raise issues for anyone who has ever struggled to work a new idea through a traditional organization. And they haunt all organizations needing fresh thoughts to survive.

Businesses everywhere are exploring ways to liberate ideas. It is interesting that the subject is inevitably tackled in lovely settings away from work, with colorful speakers, artists, entertainers, and other "creatives" (one of my least favorite terms) at events called "retreats." Creativity needs to be dealt with *at work*, however, in events we should call "advances."

Countless books, management seminars, and graduate school programs concern themselves with the problem of finding means of adjusting, opening, and otherwise making room for innovative thinking within traditional organizations. While there is value in many of the emerging ideas, they simply do not go far enough or deep enough to have lasting impact.

This book will turn the problem on its head. Making room within an organization for creativity is one thing. Designing an organization around creativity itself is quite another. This is not simply to advocate an increase of the role of creativity *in* business. It is to advocate creativity as the principal role *of* business.

This simple-sounding but far-reaching shift demands a complete rethinking of some of the most well-accepted principles and fundamentals of organizational design and management. It is not that corporations need to disassemble structures already in place, but rather that they must approach and utilize them in fresh ways. Many areas traditionally considered troublesome and even destructive will be found surprisingly conducive to imaginative thought. When creativity is prioritized as the central organizing principle in business, not only is the likelihood of innovation increased, but the more usual concerns such as productivity, efficiency, quality control, team spirit, and sales are also enhanced. The resulting atmosphere, while challenging and stimulating, also becomes supportive and humane, since a workplace safe for ideas is a workplace safe for people.

After more than a decade of experience with the Big Three

automakers of Detroit, I and a small group of automobile designers, engineers, and modelers committed ourselves to developing a new organization specifically around the needs and priorities of the creative process. While at first we had little grasp of either the challenges or full implications of this experiment, we gradually discovered several powerful, often unorthodox, managerial strategies and organizational design principles that had potentially broad application well beyond the concerns of our new enterprise.

Creative leaps often emerge from the ambiguous gaps between familiar but disparate zones of understanding. And they typically require an abrupt disengagement, a sudden shift in perspective providing a separation from things-as-they-are. The opportunity for just such a dramatic gap and dislocation came when the phone rang on that bone-chilling winter's day at the GM Tech Center, and it would permanently change the way I thought about and did business.

***

On a windswept site about a half mile inland from the Pacific, adjacent to the University of California at San Diego, and in the middle of the city's rapidly growing high-tech district, we selected an architect, Ken Ronchetti, with whom we felt great simpatico, and began designing a stunning facility. San Diego was selected as the home for NDI as much because an automobile had never been designed or built there as for its natural beauty and great climate. A core group of exceptionally gifted designers, engineers, modelers, and prototype makers was assembled and, with a completely fresh start in an ideal setting, work commenced to realize the president of Nissan's dream of "the world's most creative design satellite."

While the new building was being completed, we rented a temporary space, and with one large warehouse room to occupy, began designing cars for Nissan. Unlike the setup in Japan, where each discipline enjoyed its own separate space, NDI began life as a cauldron of boiling and colliding cultures abrading against one another's workstyles, rhythms, and priorities. It all felt like design school again, the slightly sulfurous, humid smell of warm modeling clay mingling with the sweet aroma of freshly cut wood templates. Sketches were tacked up, helter-skelter, on any available surface. The engineers fought desperately to clear out and guard their own necessarily clean areas from the inks, paints, tape, and other detritus of the creative design process. Everything was discussed by everyone, and the atmosphere was noisy, intense, irreverent, and by turns joyous and abrasive.

Most of the raw elements of a truly creative environment were in place as we began designing Nissan's line of light trucks, our first major assignment. In the scramble to cover an assignment that was larger than our staff could comfortably handle at the time, every-

one's work was stretched beyond their job descriptions, and disciplines overlapped. The designers, engineers, and modelers all got into one another's turf. We applied ourselves with intensity, often literally working around the clock. But we also took sudden breaks together, stopping work entirely for brief periods of inspired lunacy. We began taking play seriously at work.

There was an exhilaration at shedding some of the constricting rituals and assumptions of Detroit's aging design process, along with our no-longer-obligatory suits and ties. But we were far more certain about what we no longer wanted to do than we were about how to achieve what we wanted. Nonetheless, we were committed to our goal of building the company around the needs of creative thinking, and by a process of instinct and self-observation, trial and error, proceeded in a spirit consistent with creative discovery itself.

Linda, who seems to weave in an out of this journey at pivotal moments, is an organizational and clinical psychologist, and at the time was enlightening various companies for whom she was consulting about the dangers of unrecognized stress. One evening she brought home a little plastic card with a silvered square impregnated on it. When held between thumb and forefinger for about a minute, it shifted to one of four colors. If, when the finger was removed, it was blue, you were stress-free; if green, in mild but productive stress; if red, in the danger zone; and if black, you were in the soup. She asked if I'd like to try it. Given the fun I was having, as well as the liberation I felt at work, I was sure I'd register a serene sky blue.

When I lifted my thumb from the card, I had to check to see if I had inadvertently dipped it in India ink. I had left a virtual black hole. I brought the card to work the next day, and after testing everyone, to my surprise found that we all registered between infrared and pitch-black. All the overlapping, abrading, and colliding of diverse disciplines, while yielding a tremendous amount of energy, heat, and innovation, was also generating an unexpected level of conflict and stress.

With the additional complexities of two foreign cultures rubbing shoulders in an intimate, charged atmosphere, a situation arose which might easily have led to deep misunderstanding and a perceived need for tight, traditional controls. This is precisely the case with most foreign subsidiaries, which tend to be constrained and dominated by the culture of the parent company, and it is also true of diverse corporations yoked together in new mergers. But the president and key executives of Nissan remained true to their word and accommodated, even protected, the autonomy of their fledgling satellite.

With an unusual mandate to evolve our own culture in order to realize authentically "Western" design, the situation served as a catalyst to rethink the relationship between creativity and business. Furthermore, Nissan was dissatisfied with its own level of creative design and eager to learn from its new satellite.

While these early years were exhilarating and truly did feel like recess, it was clear that simply prioritizing creativity had not created a playground. What we had created, however, was a field of fertile imagination. Without losing this spirit, we wanted now to learn how to manage and harness it. The energy of the creative nucleus was beginning to form a new field around itself.

When negotiating with the various departments of the parent company, we never lost sight of our priority. It began to serve as a guide, a steady compass-setting during a turbulent period, and affected both the form and content of our dialogue. We took great pains to explain NDI's emerging methodology to a highly inquisitive people, a process that further sharpened our own understanding of it. Nissan was fascinated, and as a result, we began to see that the creative model might have significance beyond our own organization and application to broader corporate interactions.

Of course, merely raising the elements of creative methodology as issues to be taken seriously in corporate interactions did not transform all departments into innovation machines. But their insertion into the discourse brought new dimensions to the table and began to elevate levels of awareness, sensitivity, and responsiveness.

While creative individuals have received considerable attention among psychologists and organizational consultants, those with the gift of spotting significant new ideas, or at least the capacity to tolerate the discomfort they initially provoke, are rare and equally vital to the process. Corporations will dole out small fortunes to hire consultants or "creative stars," having failed to recognize the seeds of homegrown innovation all around them. Behind every corporate breakthrough is someone in authority who recognized, supported, and ultimately had the courage to use it. Our continual discussions of the evolving process of innovative thinking at NDI helped the corporation to see that they as well as we were critical to producing new ideas for Nissan. Creative expression is a bipolar event; it requires both a sender and a receiver. And its prioritization is as dependent upon the antennae of a corporation as its transmitters.

Unprecedented thinking often involves the holding of apparently disconnected, conflicting, overlapping, or even mutually exclusive thoughts in the mind simultaneously. By substituting the words "people" or "groups" for "thoughts" in the previous sentence, it is possible to see creativity's potential as an organizing force for relationships as well as for information. In this way, the shadow cast by two strongly divergent orientations is rendered irrelevant in the blinding light of their possible fusion into an utterly original perspective. And the differences between abrading disciplines can generate bold new concepts in that conflicted no-man's-land of overlapping responsibilities, a region blessed with as much potential for breakthrough as for conflict.

✳ ✳ ✳

Over time, eleven key strategies emerged from the creative imperative. They did not arise from theory. Rather, they grew from the exigencies of maintaining the direction in which we cast ourselves. Following that direction and doing what was necessary to maintain it were consistent with important aspects of the creative process itself, a process more closely connected to search than to re-search.

When the first whiff of an idea comes to light I experience a split second of pure, limpid clarity, a sense of lift accompanied by a surge of energy. The notion itself seems to arrive with a life force of its own, some innate, self-organizing inertia that begins signaling back to me what steps to take next. And so, ironically, one of the unexpected requirements of being creative is having the courage to be passive at such moments, to allow the nascent idea to assume the lead as well as the form it needs to take. There is exquisite joy to be had at these times, but also trepidation and unease at relinquishing control while being led into uncharted territories.

It was in this fashion that we submitted ourselves to evolving the priorities of the creative process at NDI. Over time, they became our organizational guidelines and corporate mythologies. Although the following chapters will describe them in a clear and discrete fashion, this was not the manner or even necessarily the order in which they were born. Ideas most often come into being in a nonlinear manner, with associations and disparate notions simultaneously overlapping, colliding, and suddenly congealing into a new whole. The birth of the priorities was a pretty messy business, and I hope I've left enough of the vital hit-and-miss struggle and necessary experimentation in the tales and anecdotes that follow.

Some of these strategies seemed to appear in full flower, others struggled for years to take shape, while still others required continual redefinition, regeneration, and rebirth. But gradually, with continual adjustment, experiment, and discussion, they began to take coherent form. And they worked!

The operating principles described in the following chapters are not reserved for creative departments or businesses such as design studios, film crews, or ad agencies. This book proposes a far deeper, more wide-ranging application, both at the heart of a corporation and across its departmental borders, so that it might become a fertile ground—rather than a burial ground—for nourishing and growing innovative ideas. It is in the gaps, voids, and overlapping zones of activity that they have their greatest impact.

Many of these creative priorities are surprising, and some might at first seem counterintuitive to accepted notions of sound business practices. They are extremely varied in tone and content, but in scanning over them, four themes emerge as common to them all: issues of *polarity*, issues of the *boundary*, the elements of *unprecedented thinking*, and a focus on *synthesis*.

Further consideration reveals these four as facets of a singularity that defines the creative orientation.

Polarities are the opposites, inconsistencies, discontinuities, and ambiguities that ignite the creative spark. I have found that, rather than being stifled by discomforting, seemingly antagonistic positions, imaginative thought flourishes in their midst. While Arthur Koestler and others have recognized the role of disconnected planes of thought in creative ideation, the *creative priority* extends their impact into the realm of human interaction and creative collaboration.

Unprecedented thinking expands the limits of what constitutes appropriate, responsible, reliable, and intelligent thought beyond the strictures of the scientific method. It engages the logical with the emotional, the scientific with the aesthetic. It requires reorientation and disorientation. It reengages the instinctive creative capacities of the unschooled child and, like the child, uses the fruits of failure and play. And it is as vitally concerned as the child with questions of why, and with how questions themselves are asked.

Boundaries are the lines between disconnected planes of thought. Making them, clarifying them, and protecting them have been a principal preoccupation of business as well as education and society. Creative activity, however, does not confine itself to in-bounds play. It comes to life at the edges, whether by blurring, abrading, overlapping, or breaking through the partitions. The *creative priority* embraces and utilizes the chasms and the barriers that separate departments, disciplines, cultures, personalities, and zones of responsibility.

It is perhaps the last theme, *synthesis*, that is most lacking in corporate thinking. Synthesis is the principal impulse of the act of creation. In a world obsessed with analysis, with the taking apart of things and issues into their component parts, creativity is the impulse to integrate, unify, and bring together. It tolerates (and at the early stages even prefers) higher levels of disorder and disintegration so that it can reorder at newer and higher levels of integration. Far too little has been learned about the powerful mental muscles required to bring everything together into a coherent whole, a vital capability needed to cope with the growing complexities of the world of business and of the world itself.

The following chapters will organize eleven key strategies for attaining and maintaining the *creative priority* according to these four principal themes. Each strategy, however, will serve to illustrate facets of the others. It is in the nature of synthesized, creative thought that each part is intricately interrelated to all the others.

PART I

Polarity

The opposite of a correct statement is a false statement. But the opposite of a profound truth may well be another profound truth.

Neils Bohr[1]

1

Creative Abrasion

NDI was born in an atmosphere rife with abrasion. One culture had joined another for help in an area in which it was particularly uncomfortable: the breaking of traditions. A varied group of disciplines had been gathered closely together, each with its own aspirations for what the enterprise might become. I'd left a familiar, comfortable relationship with an established corporation to help found a new entity with strangers in an unfamiliar setting. And from Detroit's perspective, I was seen as having joined "the enemy," switching sides in an economic war between America and Japan. Clearly, this was not going to be a serene retreat for quiet meditation.

Friction between individuals and groups is typically thought of as something harmful. And it usually is. It generates heat and discomfort, disrupts interactions, and can destroy relationships. Between a couple it can lead to divorce. Between countries it can lead to war. Within corporations it can distort and disrupt communication and ruin cohesiveness. Businesses of all types spend considerable time and money trying to reduce or eliminate it. In human terms, it is surely one of the most plentiful and volatile sources of energy on the planet.

While the early years at NDI were disruptive and chafing, however, they were also exciting and explosively fertile. And since creative output was critical, we needed to find ways to reduce the friction without destroying the very ingredients that might be essential to the vibrancy of the process; without, in other words, disrupting our disruptiveness. Multiple disciplines in the same studio, fights over what radio stations to listen to, divergent perceptions of appropriate work hours, modes of dress, codes of behavior, even what was perceived as quality work . . . all of this I saw as a rich and yeasty opportunity for a kind of friction I wanted to turn into light rather than heat. The uneasiness in my stomach and the fireworks in my brain told me there was some vital connection between the abrasiveness itself and original thinking. If we could grasp this connection, we would be tapping into a vast reservoir of creative energy.

***

The room was tense as a group of Japanese engineers and planners confronted a team of American designers across a drawing-littered conference table. The vehicle we had been laboring on for almost a year, the first-generation Nissan Pathfinder, was in its concluding developmental phase and was bristling with challenging innovations and new forms. It was to mark Nissan's first entry into the emerging off-road SUV (sport utility vehicle) market in America.

To the Japanese at the time, the imagined uses and romantic appeal of this sport/utility hybrid appeared nearly incomprehensible. The forms of the existing American versions seemed terribly bold, even rude to their eyes. And the very notion of wanting to go "off-road," of spontaneously breaking with the pack, simply turning off a legally marked driving pathway to explore unmarked territory on an impulse was unthinkable to this eminently law-abiding people. To the engineers, among the most cautious of a well-guarded population, the whole project felt uncomfortably Western, as in the Wild West, and very alien.

Although to our eyes we had fashioned a rather civilized, urbane variant of the genre, to Japanese eyes the forms NDI had modeled appeared audacious and rough-hewn. The fenders swelled with highly characterized "bulging triceps" around each wheel. Inspired by the protective structure of the roll bar jutting up from behind the front seats of jeeps and other military vehicles in the event of rollover on extremely rough surfaces, the Pathfinder integrated this extra bracing into the very skin of the vehicle itself. The diagonal struts strengthening the body pillar behind the front door framed the unusual triangular vent windows that appeared behind the front-door glass in the two-door version, and that provided badly needed ventilation for the rear passenger compartment.

Pathfinder integrated roll bar, triangular vent window, and "bulging tricep" fender forms

Understandably, the Japanese planners and engineers wanted to grasp as much as possible of the thinking behind this challenging new design. By being even more thorough than usual, they provided themselves with some badly needed feelings of security and confidence in their task. Meanwhile, the American staff felt intuitively certain they had gotten hold of a truly fresh and appropriate interpretation for this kind of car and were eager to see it realized.

Each side was pushing hard and the groups had reached an impasse on the resolution of a variety of difficult issues. The project was running late due to a growing, almost obsessive need on the part of the Japanese to restudy, research, and refine every detail. In a moment of frustration at the meeting I said, "Gentlemen, aspects of this design are truly new, and if we don't get it to market soon, we simply won't be *first!*"

The *shukan* (project leader) leaned forward, somewhat agitated, and responded, "But Hirshberg-san, we were thinking about being *best!*"

There was an abrupt, suspended silence. The Americans looked at the Japanese, then each other, and no one moved to fill the silence or bridge the gap. What had been laid bare, exposed in its purest form, were two inarguable, fundamentally alien points of view embedded deeply in each of these cultures.

Some dawning instinct urged me to step back from the moment rather than debate "first" versus "best." I thanked the Japanese for sharing their concerns and suggested that the meeting be concluded at that point. Each group left with these dual polarities nagging and pulling at each other, like the flip-flopping images in a reversible figure/ground illusion, neither prevailing for long and nearly impossible to perceive simultaneously. In the ensuing days and weeks, however, the Japanese moved with dispatch to resolve the remaining issues while the Americans refined their concepts, double-checking every new aspect with painstaking thoroughness. Neither gave up its principal goal, but each now more fully comprehended the concerns and motivations of the other. With subtle but profoundly broadened ends in mind, the vehicle concluded in a reasonably brief period of time, all innovations included and questions fully resolved.

***

Perhaps the most novel and all-encompassing management and interaction process to emerge from prioritizing creativity, I called this concept *creative abrasion*. It evolved from an understanding of innovative thinking best described by the scientist/educator/ writer Arthur Koestler as "the sudden interlocking of two previously unrelated skills or matrices of thought."[1] And it grew out of an urgent need to deal with an atmosphere of colliding cultures as well as the natural friction from the interaction of broadly varied personalities and viewpoints. Just as the creative fusion of ideas can occur by holding seemingly antithetical thoughts in the mind simultaneously, so creative collaboration between people can occur by an effort to retain conflicting cultural and disciplinary viewpoints in the mind *without discarding or allowing either to dominate*.

Conventional strategies to reduce friction by compromising, diluting, or aligning positions are the equivalent of getting all the parts in a system moving in the same direction. That's a fine procedure for rowing a boat; not so fine for creating one. *Creative abrasion* recognizes the positive dimensions of friction, the requisite role it plays in making things *go*. Without it, engines would not work, a crucial source of heat and electricity would be eliminated, and relative motion across the surface of the planet would all but cease. Rather than trying to reduce the friction that naturally arises between people working together by diluting or compromising positions, *creative abrasion* calls for the development of leadership styles that focus on first identifying and then incorporating polarized viewpoints. In doing so, the probabilities for unexpected juxtapositions are sharply increased, as are the levels of mutual understanding. The irony is that out of a process keyed on abrasiveness, a corporate culture of heightened sensitivity and harmony is achieved.

Of course, not all abrasive situations have creative potential, and the process is a learned skill. After hearing about this concept at a meeting at NDI, a group of executives from Salomon, the great French ski equipment manufacturer, attempted to apply it. When they returned to San Diego from France a few months later for a design review of the ski boot concepts we were developing for them, one of the vice presidents said, "Well, we have the abrasion part down pat!"

Recognizing, marking, and transforming pregnant moments of friction and collision into opportunities for breakthroughs are the work of *creative abrasion*. One event leaps to mind as a dramatic example of this work, since it resulted in a design that became a visual expression of the process itself.

* * *

Contentious meetings are always more interesting than smooth, efficient ones, but they generally produce little more than heat, sour stomachs, and good gossip. One such meeting occurred at the Los Angeles headquarters for Nissan Sales and Marketing. About a dozen top planning, engineering, marketing, and sales executives from Japan and America had gathered to discuss long-range plans for the product lineup in this country. I was the sole design representative, and happy to be included. In laying out guidelines and underlying assumptions, the statement was made that "all inexpensive entry-level vehicles should be generic in character." Highly distinctive, innovative design, it was further assumed, should be reserved for pricier offerings. This amounted to saying that anyone interested in a cost-effective purchase was somehow devoid of taste or discrimination. I saw red, but contained myself verbally, if not through body language. "Why do we assume that to be the case?" I asked. "It's self-evident," was the reply. "Not to me, but I won't argue this point in your language." I intended to come back to the next meeting, to be held a few months hence, with a rebuttal in design terms.

The meeting had provided a powerful source of abrasion with a set of assumptions that simply "rubbed me the wrong way." Each discipline and culture brought its own viewpoints and priorities to the table. The engineers tended to think of design as something added to a product. Less of it, surely, would reduce the cost of an entry-level vehicle. The marketers and planners at the time thought of design as existing in stratified levels, consistent with the way they'd conceptualized the market, with the undifferentiated masses at the bottom ascending up through the ranks to the highly differentiated elite at the top. Hence, such needlessly pricey and trivial concepts as "designer" jeans, homes, and cars. And the Japanese, with their even more stratified society, had traditionally equated inexpensive, mass-market products with ordinary, commonplace design. To the designer, who perhaps naively believes every product has its own inherent truth, some soul to be expressed, these are confining, even threatening words.

By refusing to engage in a linear, across-the-table debate on the same plane of thought, however, I had forced the discussion to another plane; in this case a visual one. The potential had now increased for the abrading situation to "rub me the right way."

Like many others, whenever I take a trip by car or leave ground in a plane, I experience mental liftoff. The minute I got into my car after the meeting to return to San Diego, I was suddenly alert to a host of images and visual metaphors that flashed into my mind, all ignited by the abrasive remarks of the discussion. For reasons I did not yet understand, two images that flickered onto my mental screen caught my immediate attention: a grasshopper and a Bell helicopter! A third image joined these two a split second later: a truck, surely (at the time) the most humble, generic, and "dumbed-down" of all entry-level products. All at once, the three images coalesced, and a vision of a truck unlike any I'd ever seen assembled itself. It was as if a sports car had been rear-ended by a careening, loose truck bed, the two gracelessly jammed together and looking for all the world like some kind of helicopter on wheels. I pulled off Route 405 at the next exit and crudely sketched the image on a legal pad before it evaporated from my mind.

When I returned to NDI, I gathered a group of engineers, modelers, and designers around and shared my experience of the meeting, the abrasion, and the rough sketch that it triggered. Everyone was appalled by the "entry-level" comment, and immediately attracted to the design rebuttal. Although we had a full slate of assigned projects at the time, an ad hoc team of anyone interested was assembled, and in less than two months a one-fourth-scale clay model was finished, along with engineering drawings showing how the vehicle could easily and cheaply be built using most of the components from our existing Hardbody trucks.

I eventually realized it was the blunt audacity of the abruptly joined forms of the grasshopper and helicopter that caused them to emerge from a lifetime file of stored images. These were humble things designed for clear purposes. Each of their separate parts expressed a discrete function with naked, unapologetic directness.

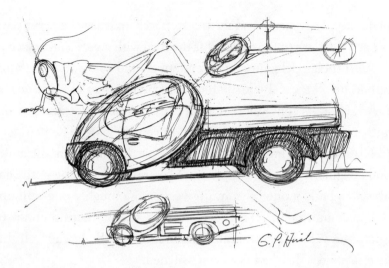

Original Gobi concept sketch by the author

This insect and insect-like thing constituted a pair of unmistakable and unforgettable icons.

A truck, too, is a humble thing with clear purposes. My original crude sketch identified it as an object with two clear functional zones: a forward box for carrying people; a rearward box for carrying things. So a helicopter-like, grasshoppery truck began to develop in the studios at NDI. But it was what the staff did with the concept that brought it to life.

Innovations erupted everywhere at once. A theme of bold juxtapositions of form and texture was carried throughout the vehicle. An egg-like, ovoid shell for passenger and driver was rudely intersected by a corrugated cargo bed, the doorcut undulating to further demarcate the line of intersection. Two pairs of storage pods were located beneath the bed; on the driver's side they were labeled "stuff" and "things"; on the passenger side, "odds" and "ends." The interior was starkly divided into a driver's cockpit and a more open, flexible passenger zone. The glove box became an easily detachable canvas carrying bag held in place by Velcro. The front grille was simply an area of perforated sheet metal, and the truck's "face" smiled at the world years before Chrysler's smiling Neon hit the road with a very similar face.

With the model painted in a variety of bold colors to further differentiate all the vehicle's parts, I returned to the next meeting in L.A., and at its conclusion, dramatically undraped it. It was greeted with a chorus of surprised smiles and even applause. The president of Nissan at the time, Yukata Kume, a particularly bold, dynamic, and imaginative leader, happened to be present, and gave us the go-ahead to build a one-off running version—a roughly one-million-dollar commitment. He also instructed the marketing group to clinic the vehicle's potential as an addition to the lineup. All this from a project that had not been assigned.

The truck was named the Gobi and was introduced at the Detroit International Auto Show in 1990. It traveled the international circuit for over three years, accruing countless awards and acclaim, including Car of the Show in Detroit, the Gold Medal from the Industrial Designers Society of America, and *Time* magazine's Transportation Product of the Year in 1990. Several films about it were made, including a European documentary on its conception by the renowned filmmakers Eila Hershon and Roberto Guerra and released around the world in several languages.[2]

The vehicle was never mass-produced, however. The clinics had found, to no great surprise, that the design polarized opinion. Furthermore, the early nineties were a time of increasingly sensitive trade and economic issues between Japan and America, and it was not deemed a wise moment to expand the product line. Nevertheless, the Gobi was probably the single most impactful car Nissan never manufactured. Alex Taylor of *Fortune* magazine called it at the time the "finest unbuilt vehicle in the world."

While disappointed the car was never released for sale, we were nonetheless gratified that the project introduced the language of design into the corporate strategy dialogue. It had a profound impact on the way Nissan (and other corporations) thought about trucks, entry-level vehicles, design, and the market.

All these positive results flowed from a concept born of friction and disagreement. Creativity and destructiveness are at the same time polar opposites and closely related cousins. Every precocious kindergartner knows the sense of liberation from toppling a carefully constructed tower of blocks in order to make room for the next one. Innovation requires the capacity to disdain tradition and break with comfortable routines and mastered skills. This is precisely why it can be uncomfortable when first confronting something genuinely new. "[E]ven the creators of new scientific ideas often find their offspring unbearable."[3]

With its jazzy, highly contrasted, and boldly juxtaposed elements, the Gobi clearly expressed the very nature of the process that produced it: *creative abrasion*. Although fueled at its inception by negative energy, it became infused with an optimistic spirit, one that challenged established customs and knocked over some blocks, with a smile and a wink.

Gobi prototype

***

Japan, with its deep love and respect for tradition, places a high priority on honoring and working within them. And it enjoys all the societal benefits that flow from a shared, living heritage. It also struggles deeply when confronted with change and the need to depart from custom. America, on the other hand, has at best a passing regard for tradition, having been born out of the need to escape existing ones. If it shares any tradition, it is the common capacity to break them! And, of course, it suffers all the societal woes of a rule-breaking culture. It also benefits from the freedom to continually reinvent itself and create new traditions. And it more readily accommodates change. There are great gifts and equally great costs that flow from either way of being in the world, but NDI seems to gain from the uneasy and sometimes abrasive coexistence of both in its bicultural makeup.

The prioritization of creativity requires the accommodation of dissent from the prevailing view. While this does not automatically lead to unprecedented thinking, it does open the corporate arteries to the flow of new thoughts. But it requires a tolerance for some real and often threatening discomfort. The abrasion *of creative abrasion* is truly abrasive! It must be, or there would be no challenge to established modes of thought and no opportunity for unprecedented ones.

While a spark from the abutment of a dramatically polarized set of positions can enkindle the energies of new formulations, these can also be fashioned from the continual chafing of subtly differentiated outlooks over long periods of time.

❊❊❊

Nothing is more heartening or stimulating than walking into a design studio and seeing modeler/designer teams huddled intimately around developing prototypes. While the designer is supposed to be responsible for the concept, its realization into three dimensions relies on the interpretive and re-creative skills of the modeler. With an incomplete, still-forming image in his/her mind's eye at the earliest stages of the conceptualization process, the designer must find ways to objectify it, to communicate it to the sculptor by any means possible.

Sketches, cross-sectional drawings, designspeak, and all manner of hand waving and body gesturing fill the atmosphere and clutter the work surface around the emerging clay model. The modeler has to find a way to "read" these articulations and give palpable form to the embryonic glimmers they represent. The ensuing give-and-take is at once tentative and passionate, searching yet committed to an imagined direction. Together, modeler and designer circle the amorphous, infinitely malleable clay, considering its forms from up close and afar, stooping, squinting, and working it from all angles. They engage in a kind of intimate creativity dance to a music and a beat not yet fully realized or clearly heard. Images come to mind of Renaissance creators, collaborating intensively with highly skilled artisans and apprentices to realize their far-flung visions.

But these interactions are often anything but cordial. Modelers, like designers, are usually graduates of fine arts schools or university art departments, and most have degrees in sculpture, pottery-making, or other crafts. As is characteristic of persons capable of thinking not only visually but three-dimensionally, they can often be quite creative. Yet, in most design studios the modeler is restrained from engaging in the creative conceptualization process. In Detroit, to make matters worse, since the modelers are unionized, a designer cannot even touch the clay, as it is considered in violation of the prescribed division of labor. General Motors' solution to the frequent collision of imaginations in working out ideas was generally to make a clean break between the responsibilities of those two disciplines; the designers were to create, the modelers to interpret.

One of the organizational aspects of Detroit design practice we most wanted to leave behind was this artificial division and limiting of innovative input. With the application of a strategy called *blur-*

ring the boundaries (to be discussed in Chapter 7), NDI elected to exacerbate the built-in friction of this relationship by deliberately overlapping the responsibilities of designers and modelers. If modelers had ideas, why, we wondered, should we not use them? The strategy, of course, was fraught with perils, like those concerning multiple creative chefs cooking up one dish. But as with so many other dimensions of the creative priority, we elected to hold fast to our path and work out the issues as we went along.

Effecting this change, however, has not been easy. A certain amount of resistance was expected from some of the designers, but a considerable portion has come from an unexpected source, the modelers themselves. Since traditionally they were considered makers of things, not ideas, there was a tendency to consider the clay model as an object, a thing-unto-itself rather than a three-dimensional representation of an evolving concept, a work-in-progress. In such a context, the modeler served as a skilled craftsperson, an extension of the designers' hands, and was therefore judged by the quality of the model, its level of finish, refinement, and perfection. Standards of evaluation and zones of responsibility were clear, familiar, and comfortable. As the model (and the modeler) gradually became a more active and integral part of the creative process, however, these standards and zones became fuzzy, and the sources for abrasion abounded.

After investing weeks in crafting and refining the clay, for example, the modelers tended to feel personally rebuked by critical comments at reviews. The designers insisted they were commenting on the concepts, not their execution. "But how do you separate an idea from its execution?" wondered Don Sondys, a highly conscientious modeler. "Even if it's announced that the refinement and detailing of the model are not the issue," he continued, "that's simply not possible. A review of a visible object is just that, and people will ultimately react to what they see in front of them."

Still, Sondys fully realized the value of checking out the concept, the broad direction. Everyone seemed of split mind about the sub-ject, and the discussions as well as the abrasion went on, unre-solved, for years.

Al Holgerson, NDI's senior modeler and an accomplished sculp-tor and pottery-maker in his own right, was agitated and increas-ingly uncomfortable with this situation. Attracted to the company in the first place by its promise of a more open and inclusive involvement in the creative process, he did not yet see a substan-tively changed methodology to accommodate it. Too much time, he felt, was being wasted perfecting the surfaces to the same degree throughout the process, only to see them rejected and discarded due to weaknesses inherent in the concept itself.

The problem, he reasoned, lay more with the modelers than the designers. They had continued to regard their work in a monolithic fashion, treating each stage essentially the same. While they were enjoying a new freedom in expressing their opinions and hunches at NDI, they were not yet using modeling as an active part of the creative search.

Holgerson liked to boil issues, as well as forms, down to their sim-plest elements before working them out. He would sit in front of the clay, zen-like, for considerable lengths of time before touching it with his tools, working out his moves like an Olympic diver before executing them. While some modelers preferred building up the forms step by step, he was able to intuit the overall gesture of a design almost immediately. Observing him beginning a model was like watching a particularly gifted caricaturist capture the essential elements of a likeness with the first few strokes of charcoal.

Why wouldn't it be possible, he wondered, to briefly freeze the model at this rough, gestural phase and call for a concept review? That is exactly what he did, and after informing everyone at an out-door critique what his quickly done model represented, the review proceeded with great effectiveness.

The idea and its implications gradually spread throughout the building, sparking new controversies. Everyone seemed to hold conflicting points of view, often embraced by the same individuals. Diane Allen, chief designer, immediately liked being able to see her ideas more quickly. "I feel I can try more things, and I tend now to make each stroke count," she said. "On the other hand," she continued, "I worry some about a feeling of being rushed, of needing to hurry. My new ideas are like baby chicks . . . some need more incubation time than others."

Jim McJunkin, a meticulous designer from Texas, felt that "God is in the details and the nuances, and these take time to resolve." Chris Lee, a Korean-American designer, agreed, and further worried that "strange, challenging new directions become more acceptable only after brought to a certain level of finish." But McJunkin then countered himself with the observation, "I like the imposed haste. I'm a perfectionist, and it's a nice counterbalance to my workstyle. And," he continued, "there's something provocative in the unfinished-ness of the models," a statement that implicitly acknowledged the added value of the modelers' creative instincts in these spontaneous interpretations.

"If the model's not worth a damn, the reviews are meaningless!" warned Larry Brinker, the head of NDI's entire modeling effort. "But in some situations and for some of the designers, I can see how it can be helpful," he suggested, thereby refusing to impose his concerns on the whole group.

Armando Palomares, a Hispanic-American modeler, liked the impact on the designers of the "two-day model" or "speedform," as it was now being called. "They don't get as fixated on any one direction," he said, smiling, "and many now work on several simultaneously. It's exhausting, but it gets the juices flowing and I definitely feel like more of a partner in the process."

"Hell," stated Arthur Markievicz with characteristic bluntness, "I have no interest whatsoever in having to help create the idea. That's the designer's headache!" And so it went, the debate and the stimulating chafing kept alive by the varying workstyles and approaches.

But by staying our course, resisting the urge to immediately relieve the agitation and still the debate, the scope and nature of NDI's modeling efforts gradually altered and expanded. A highly intuitive, concept-evaluating dimension had come into existence, one requiring new skills from the modelers and new ways of seeing, judging, and using the model by the designers. And it offered further opportunities for creative input to the design process by the sculptors.

Knowing how to manage an extended period of agitation so that it might yield new paths requires the development of a keen sense of timing and considerable patience on the part of management. It is a matter of intuiting when to interfere, when to step in and when to let things take their own course. There are, of course, times when an abrasive situation is leading nowhere. Certain designer/modeler teams are like oil and water, and there is no sense in letting things go past a certain point. However, even in these most discordant of pairings, we still encourage the toleration of a reasonable period of struggle, as it is often from the interaction of the most unlikely and stridently polarized positions that the greatest leaps can occur.

Creative abrasion does not always erupt from a single triggering event like the provocative meeting that led to the Gobi. It can also do its work like the infinitesimal friction of water in a creek, forging its own course and, in time, carving grand canyons.

Jim McJunkin noted that "it is the abrasion of tiny air molecules that creates the beauty of a shooting star, without which it would be just another rapidly moving, cold and anonymous piece of rock."

❋❋❋

Perceptive and agile leadership is required to recognize and mark these potent moments or periods of abrasion and collision. The energies typically squandered on defense or debate must be rechanneled into the much tougher but ultimately more rewarding work of holding the multiple viewpoints in mind simultaneously. The sparks from such interactions can shed light on wholly unexpected and new planes of thought.

Of course, companies should not set out to look for friction. A creatively abrasive atmosphere is not one filled with petty bickering, hostility, or needless turmoil. Nor is it aggressively competitive. Ideas will not only fail to survive in such a culture, they will fail to arise at all. While refocusing attention onto the creative values of intersecting streams of thought can have the effect of actually lowering stress to more manageable and productive levels, that is not the principal purpose of this strategy.

Rather, there is a need to recognize the very real opportunities and energies available when the heat and friction of abrading points of view are encountered. As in the great supercolliders used in the research of particle physics, it is precisely the managed collision of powerfully oppositional streams that releases previously untapped matter and energy. With appropriate vision, it is possible to reconfigure the corporate mechanism into a kind of creative supercollider.

2

Hiring in Divergent Pairs

As soon as I began seriously considering Nissan's offer—moments into Korn-Ferry's second call—I began thinking about who my first key hires would be. Nothing seemed more urgent or central than the hiring process itself. I did not immediately think about a vision statement (something we're going to have to get around to one of these days, hopefully after I retire). I did not imagine an organizational design, or even know where our ideal creative sandbox might be located. Since sandboxes are not conceived for solitary activity, my first question was who I might play with there.

The issues I faced at start-up were so diverse, it was hard to imagine individuals capable of handling (and enjoying) them all. Two people I'd known at GM, however, immediately leapt to mind as appealing candidates, for reasons that became clear to me over time. And the success of the simultaneous hiring of NDI's first two design managers set the pattern for a critical strategy of the *creative priority*.

***

Upon receiving an assignment to design a car, Allan Flowers would first clear out a flattish area on his desktop. With the distracted, slightly disheveled appearance of a professor/researcher in some arcane subject rather than a designer of sleek objects, he had to rearrange the mounds of notes, sketches, graphs, pencil stubs, engineering drawings, and what might possibly be something organic (potatoes? mushrooms?) growing in the shadows cast by the faint blue glow of his computer terminal. The complex business of designing an automobile began for him by visually and logically mapping out all the parts and pieces, nuts and bolts, schedules and priorities of the entire project. The new material generated by this activity joined all the residue around him from previous and ongoing projects. This included concepts for the helm station of a yacht, sketches of some odd flying machines (he now holds many of NDI's "world records" for indoor rubber-band-powered flight), wooden maquettes of minimalist sculpture, an electric, intricately articulated "walking spider" (don't ask), and other ingenious contrivances for which there are no known uses.

When handed a set of platform drawings—engineering draftings containing the basic dimensions, components, and skeletal structure of a car—by the engineers at the start of a project, Flowers rarely accepted it as presented. This was not out of contrariness, but because for him design began *before* what most (read: "engineers") thought of as doing design. Rather, he needed to start from ground zero, to understand the underlying assumptions and fully engage in that vital gray zone where engineering, planning, and design overlap.

Why, he asked, couldn't the thin seat he configured for use on a yacht be used to increase rear passenger legroom? Why couldn't the door-lock mechanism be rotated ninety degrees to accommodate flush door-glass, thereby reducing windnoise and improving aerodynamics? Such issues had a direct impact on the eventual appearance of a car. Flowers' meddling and questioning throughout the process resulted in a considerable number of design patents, and an even greater number of perplexed, but usually stimulated engineers not used to this degree of inquisitiveness about "their" areas of responsibility. The increase in innovativeness that occurred, however, triggered a rethinking of the Nissan engineering/design relationship, leading to a far more complex, interactive methodology, one which will be further elaborated in Chapter 7.

For Al Flowers, this was simply the way he needed to function. He approached design as an inventor/engineer, and found the eventual forms for his cars by playing with their parts and the process he helped shape.

When Tom Semple was confronted with an assignment, on the other hand, he would immediately begin by "cleaning house" from the previous project. His desk, taboret, markers, pastels, and pens were returned to their pristine condition, arrayed around him like an ophthalmologist's instruments before eye surgery. Eager to begin creating expressive form right away, he nonetheless listened patiently to the marketing input, scanned the engineering requirements, and read—well, glanced at—all pertinent documents. Complex graphs were a complete mystery to him (a comment not so much on the nature of his intelligence as on the grossly nonvisual nature of much of what passed for "visualized information" in corporations). He had a fundamental grasp of technological issues but was largely content to delegate their resolution to the engineers, much to their relief.

When working on the first-generation Nissan Pathfinder, one of NDI's early projects, he was determined to invest it with a level of form sophistication and detail resolution normally reserved for luxury and high-end sports cars. The swelling, flexed fenders he crafted endowed the vehicle with a muscular yet severely taut feel.

These endowed the Japanese engineers with severe headaches.

When the forms were scanned and the surface data fed to their computers, the software that had been developed in the early eighties "read" the highly complex shapes as flawed, and proceeded to automatically "correct" them.

Upon reviewing the adjusted surfaces, Semple bristled. They'd lost their muscularity, and he strongly requested they be restored to their original, "flawed" condition. Seeing the differences with their own eyes, the engineers willingly reprogrammed the computers to accept a level of form complexity they had not yet dealt with. The Pathfinder was released for production as originally designed, and went on to become NDI's first global hit, carving a unique market for itself with its distinctive (and much emulated) forms.

Semple approached design as an artist, and thought with his eyes. What he created often required ingenuity and fresh approaches in product and manufacturing development, and the engineers, inspired by the integrity of his ideas, were willing to go to extraordinary lengths to realize them. For him, invention was often the mother of necessity.

I knew that his first impulse on being asked to join NDI would be to begin designing cars. And since Nissan wanted our input from the start, I needed someone who was comfortable launching into the design process before a studio or even an organization was in place. Flowers, on the other hand, would first need to assess and establish the nature of the relationship and the product development process itself before immersing himself in it. And he would be an ideal partner for me to begin sorting through the intricacies of establishing a new, international business in a bicultural setting.

Bringing these two individuals together soon after the birth of NDI created an immediate vitality and crackling intensity. Each approached a project with utterly different priorities and workstyles. They pushed and pulled, inspired and abraded each other, one reshaping the forest by designing the trees, the other finding new forms for the trees by focusing on the forest. They proceeded as though working on different projects, which in the deepest sense, they were.

And that was the point. Every issue was addressed simultaneously from distinct orientations, which meant that NDI's organizational design as well as its products gained breadth and depth, and worked on many more planes than they might otherwise have. Furthermore, neither Semple's "styling" orientation nor Flowers' Bauhaus background became sanctified as The Corporate Methodology. As a result, both viewpoints remained available to the staff, as did a variety of hybrid versions that would later form between and beyond them.

The fortuitous coupling of Semple and Flowers, which evoked strong, often oppositional yet equally valid points of view, seemed intuitively the right thing to do. As we thought about the rest of our staffing needs, I began to seek out *pairs of divergent* designers, modelers, and engineers who, taken together, would not only meet a wider range of requirements, but also constitute a stimulating and purposefully designed mix.

***

As I left GM for my new position at NDI, I was told by executives that I should think twice about hiring a team composed solely of gifted, strong-willed individuals, especially when they did not share similar orientations. But counter to their well-meant advice, I knew that it was precisely because I did not fit their traditional mold that I had been hired by GM in the first place. Chuck Jordan, the director of styling in the early sixties, had sensed what he called a "shifting of the winds" and wanted to experiment by hiring a few non-automotive-oriented designers from atypical schools. Since we had been educated as general product designers, he felt our interaction with the staff might stimulate a broader, more open perspective.

I had expected to join one of a number of small East Coast design firms upon graduation and had told Jordan bluntly at the interview that Detroit represented for me much that was wrong with American design at the time. He caught me off guard with his response. "Look, you could go to New York and design elegant toasters that might wind up in the Modern (Museum of Modern Art) and continue to gripe about the single most important product on the planet. Or, you could give it a few years and try to impact the American automobile. We like your anger. Join us and become a paid renegade!"

I was hooked. I knew I'd be working in a place where the overwhelming percentage of my colleagues would be practicing design from a very different orientation. Not wanting to pass up this "paid renegade" opportunity, however, I set out on the job with a unique—and, I would learn, rather threatening—point of view, one that will be further explored in Chapter 9.

But, as soon became evident to me, simply hiring a few renegades to run counter to the established grain of a corporation will not alter it. Commitment to a new perspective requires deeper, more substantive adjustments at all levels. GM later made the same miscalculation on a much greater scale by bringing in Electronic Data Systems and Ross Perot. GM wanted to embrace the rapidly growing electronic world, and Perot was determined to reshape and open up their culture. Even with his Texas-sized ego and a stated intention of cutting through its layers of bureaucracy and fixed ways, he moved the behemoth not one degree, although he did manage to temporarily deplete the GM cash account upon leaving.

I left the company with a clear understanding of the dangers of a single-minded, monolithic corporate outlook, something about which they had great pride. While the ability of companies to make deep and lasting internal change is inversely proportional to their size, it is nonetheless possible. Vast corporations such as Chrysler have demonstrated that, with commitment at the top levels, dramatic shifts in character and direction can be effected. One such tectonic shift occurred when Lee Iacocca entered that company. An arguably greater one occurred when he left.

Rather than have to bring in radical perspectives or perform painful surgery from time to time in order to shake things up, I wanted to weave contrasting and complementary strands into the very fabric of NDI. It seemed to me that exceptional and varied individuals brought together with a common goal and appropriate leadership could inspire rather than intimidate each other. The least appealing kind of staff I could imagine for any business was a congregation of like-minded yea-sayers, cozy, comfortable, mutually reinforcing, and nonthreatening to top management. Achieving consensus might have been easier, but unprecedented concepts would have been far less likely. Furthermore, consensus itself is considerably more powerful when reached from different worlds via different routes.

Traditional hiring procedures, however, do not typically focus at the moment of selection on the character of the group being assembled. Instead, they concern themselves with fitting the "right person" into the available job, one at a time. But considerations of the mix, balance, and texture of the group are of critical importance when deciding whom to hire.

***

After seeing a televised war film as a child growing up in Fort Walton Beach, Florida, Robert Bauer worked out his fears through a series of precocious pencil sketches of swooping fighter jets, gun-toting soldiers, and fierce battle scenes. As with virtually all NDI's designers, he had been drawing "anything and everything" as long as he could remember. "But after reaching driving age," he told me, "mostly automobiles."

When Bauer approached NDI as a candidate, he clearly loved cars, knew cars, had built his own running cars, and from his portfolio, showed great potential for designing them. He was poised and unusually articulate for such a young designer. The work in his portfolio was bold, clearly American, and somewhat familiar in both form and presentation style. But Bauer's concepts hinted at dimensions beneath the surface. His father, a career Air Force pilot, had taught him more than just how to drive a car when he turned sixteen. He grew up with an unusual grasp of a car's inner workings, which served as a principal source of inspiration for him.

Hired by Ford upon graduation from Art Center in Pasadena, Bauer was quickly recognized for his promise, but just as quickly he felt stifled by their perception of him as a classic Detroit designer—"your pure car-guy." He left after a year and a half to join NDI's particularly open and varied atmosphere and begin the search for his own unique design voice.

An intriguing portfolio and résumé arrived from England about the same time we were considering Robert Bauer. The portfolio by Ajay (pronounced uh-JAY, with the Indian accent on the second syllable) Panchal consisted of pages crowded with dramatic sketches and illustrations of exotic car and truck forms, various products, figure drawings, and paintings. Although the style was raw and outside any currently acceptable idiom we were familiar with in America, the presentation looked for all the world like some Renaissance artist/designer's folio incongruously done in an exuberant and purely twentieth-century style.

Reinforcing this impression was one line at the conclusion of Panchal's cover letter to the portfolio proclaiming his intention to become "the Leonardo of the 21st century!" Either he had an especially dry sense of British humor, delusions of grandeur, or had found a charming way to tell us he had *very* high aspirations. Upon meeting him it was clear he had both the wit *and* the drive to excel.

As with Bauer, drawing came easy and early, as did his passion for cars. But this was no garden-variety Detroit passion. Panchal recalls a photograph of himself taken by his parents in front of the Taj Mahal on a trip to their country of origin when he was two, a prized toy bus gripped in one hand, a car in the other. He has never let go, and his zeal for shaping objects of transportation has continued unabated to this day. Unlike Bauer, however, it was never the technology of the automobile that fascinated him. Rather, it was the pure romance of sculpting the forms of objects of motion. Although Panchal had already graduated from Coventry University and been accepted (and sponsored by Ford of England) to the graduate school at the prestigious Royal College of Art in London, he felt ready to launch his career and accepted a position with NDI.

Considered separately, each of these two candidates had a good deal of potential, and some limits. Could Bauer, with his more mainstream education and orientation, derive a unique style of expression from his technological perspective and add something fresh to the mix among NDI's other "car guys"? And could Panchal ground his flights of fancy to feasible reality without losing his distinctive approach? But when we imagined how they might key off as well as balance each other's disparate backgrounds, approaches, passions, and talents, they were immediately appealing. Shortly after entering the company, these two, with no encouragement from management, became virtual sparring partners and fast friends. The debates over the differences between their approaches and philosophies often raged long into the night and stimulated many of our critiques and meetings. As a result, they have sharpened their own views, expanded the NDI design palette, and energized the rest of the staff. Together, they composed one hell of a hire.

Since with pairs-hiring, a single individual is no longer perceived as needing to fill all the requirements at any one time, we have found ourselves more open to candidates representing a significantly greater range of cognitive styles, professional approaches, and personal idiosyncrasies. Someone who might have been considered too narrowly focused might now be seen as providing an interesting counterpoint to another candidate.

The very idea of a "balanced person" as some kind of ideal has always vaguely troubled me. It is eternally associated in my mind with what high school counselors used to refer to as "well-rounded students"—shorthand for "no weirdos too deeply into their own passions." But passion about work or a particular way of working (not to be confused with the zealous need to remain identified with an ideological position) is a quality to look for in hiring, as it is an emotion closely linked to creative potential. Balance for us has now become an issue of the group rather than the individual.

Of course, it is not always possible to hire two or more people simultaneously. At these times we find it useful to mentally couple the person being considered to the most recent or next possible hire. The goal remains the same: to select and accommodate a broad and diverse cast of players for roles in dramas not yet conceived.

***

An open invitation had gone out over the loudspeaker system and virtually the entire staff had gathered outside around the Cocoon, a concept vehicle being developed by Red Studio, for a critique. Outdoor viewings were critical for evaluating the character of an emerging design. William Mitchell, the ex-VP of GM, once said, "Evaluating a car indoors is like judging a horse in a bathtub."

But we had developed some guidelines for these design reviews that made them quite unlike those we had suffered through in Detroit, where only the designers working on the model under scrutiny were invited to speak out (along with the executives), and could criticize only if they had a better solution. At NDI, the rules were: Anyone from any department in the company who was interested was welcome; if they felt the design was stupid, they were to say so; and they didn't need to have a better solution. Of course, tact was encouraged, as well as an equal willingness to openly share approval. Fostering an atmosphere safe enough for such openness required considerable effort from the managers, who had to continually reassure the staff about the value of honest, unbiased responses from those with little (or no) direct involvement in a creative task. It was well worth it.

With everyone from the janitor to the shop to administration included, the sense of participation in the principal work of the company was widespread and highly stimulating. And while there were moments of awkwardness and sometimes even pain for the designers, these were considered far less odious than the risk of discovering mistakes once the product hit the market.

Under the midday sun, every undulation and nuance of the Cocoon was thrown into mercilessly high relief, helping to focus critical attention on it. The designers who'd been working on the car stood off to one side at first, viewing the viewers with evident apprehension. They had been struggling for months on a bold but challenging design that seemed to elude their attempts to reduce some of its awkwardness and excess visual weight. Worried about losing its freshness by overreacting to the problems, they had confined themselves to making only minute adjustments. Having reached a point where they felt, or very much needed to feel, that the design was finally "coming around," they were providing each other with mutual reinforcement that everything was going to be okay.

Eventually, everyone was invited to honestly express their reactions. After a pause, someone said, "Much improved since the last show." "Not bad at all," added another. But the remarks were sparse and tepid. It all felt a bit like whistling in the dark.

Cathy Woo, an executive secretary born in China, educated in Japan and England, and now living in Southern California, only rarely spoke at such gatherings. She stood quietly sipping her tea, observing the car and the comments.

"Well, it just looks fat, dumb, and ugly to me!" she blurted out, the words in striking contrast to her characteristically courteous, almost apologetic manner. The impact was immediate. The ice had been broken. As much as everyone had wanted to acknowledge some improvement, they now admitted the car still wasn't "right."

The designers were at first stung, but a sense of relief soon followed. They had been restricting their efforts to minor, cosmetic manipulation of the forms, but now felt free to get out the scalpels and perform the major surgery required.

By the next show, the Cocoon had gelled into a powerful new statement and was ready for its premier at the Tokyo International Automobile Show. As it was being crated for shipment to Japan and the usual congratulations and acknowledgments for nearly a year's work were being issued, the designers spontaneously singled out the contribution of Ms. Woo. Her vital and gutsy comment had turned the design around at a pivotal moment.

Cathy Woo had not suddenly become a creative designer. Nor, on the other hand, was she a total stranger to the process, responding in the sterile atmosphere of a clinic. By being included and exposed to various phases of concept development, she had begun to trust her eyes and the validity of her own responses, and to become comfortable expressing her intuitive reactions.

Although hunches, inventiveness, spontaneity, ingenuity, and originality are all aspects of a truly creative act, they are not synonymous with it. If, as I sit writing this passage on a return flight from Japan, I suddenly decided to drop my pants and yodel, it would certainly be regarded by my jetlagged travelmates as a spontaneous, even an original act. But hardly a creative one. In the context, however, Ms. Woo's spontaneous utterance had played a role in the creative process.

The potential for some level of creativity exists in everyone. Contrary to popular myth, original thought is not restricted to rare individuals in isolation. It is a uniquely human enterprise that requires critics and supporters, senders and receivers, real-world grounding and unrestricted flights of the imagination. While some are clearly more predisposed than others, without a fundamental, widespread grasp of the pains and joys of birthing ideas, there would be no audience for them and no place for them to grow or be realized. By exposing and involving people such as Ms. Woo in parts of the creative process, we have found a heightened capacity for timely and incisive observations along with greater receptivity and supportiveness for new, often uncomfortable concepts when they appear. These are vital dimensions for an idea-welcoming corporate culture.

Although building business around a creative core is the organizing principle upon which *hiring in divergent pairs* is based, the increased potential for breakthrough thinking clearly does not mean targeting only creative people. Even if there existed a reliable means of identifying them (there does not), it is naive to believe that simply hiring some "idea people" will provide a company with all the originality it needs. This is akin to expecting seeds tossed on a railroad track to yield a garden there. The corporate train will prevail. Furthermore, focusing on any specific trait or talent in hiring would be inconsistent with the principle itself.

❋❋❋

The pivotal distinction between traditional hiring considerations and those surrounding *hiring in divergent pairs* is perhaps best exemplified by the differences in thinking about whom to invite to a dinner party as opposed to deciding how to organize people to make for interesting tables. The issues attending the latter are far more complex and significant (providing there are not too many family members involved) than those involved in deciding on the "right" people to invite. This shift in emphasis amounts to being more concerned with creating a stimulating party than compiling the proper guest list.

Considering individuals one by one prioritizes the job description as the principal guide, so it is natural to lean toward those with a balance of traits most closely matching it. But there is a bias in this procedure toward people who appear to fit and who represent a comfortable choice. "Comfort" here is synonymous with terms like "familiar" and "expected," and in any organization prizing original thought, familiarity and expectedness are not always desirable goals. As I had seen at GM, companies tend to return to the same sources and schools for a reliably acceptable kind of candidate. Over time, corporate meetings begin to look like alumni gatherings, hardly the most stimulating format imaginable for innovative thinking.

Current hiring procedures both buttress and homogenize the existing character and orientation of a company, but they do not necessarily strengthen it in the long run. The whole purpose of hiring is expansion, which tends to be regarded quantitatively; that is, how many people are being added. But there is a qualitative connotation to expansion that is far more important—the enlargement of the range of a company's capabilities and the breadth of its vision.

We've all had the experience as children on playgrounds and in classrooms of being both fascinated and incredulous as someone approached a common task—creating a game, tackling a math problem, building a fort—in a previously unimagined and utterly alien way. And we certainly didn't realize at the time that our own instinctive approach was probably also a source of surprise and stimulation to some of the other kids.

The minute we tentatively reach out to think or work or even question in alien ways, we are entering a region where unexpected distinctions and connections might occur. It is an unfamiliar space, not prescribed or delineated by the limits of an all-too-familiar modus operandi. And it is this very ambiguity that makes room for the sudden emergence of a potentially new order.

This is the zone of creative interaction that is being tapped by *hiring in divergent pairs*. We have all played there and learned there. Now we need to discover how to work there.

3

Embracing the Dragon

In the early nineties, both Japanese and American automobile companies were increasingly looking for new ways to reduce the extravagant expenditures they had become used to during the eighties. One obvious means of reducing the cost of manufacturing, parts, and distribution on a grand scale was to develop vehicles whose appeal crossed all cultural boundaries—global cars. The parent company requested that NDI study this issue and respond in the form of a report and a recommendation.

Instinctively, the design staff shrunk back in horror. They knew that, for most corporations, the phrase "global car" was shorthand for "mass taste," designs which would offend (or strongly attract) no one. Rather than immediately send back a sternly negative reply, however, everyone gathered together for an NDI mindmap session, an opportunity to vent and free-associate around an issue.

Most companies have meetings to deal with such questions. But meetings are not neutral mechanisms. They have built-in routines and sets of expectations. Their primary purpose is to share information and rubber-stamp decisions, which are generally made at pre-meeting meetings or postmeeting meetings. Attendees are expected to be prepared to give reports or listen to them, take notes, and follow an agenda as well as a leader. Debate is expected and the meeting's end is inevitably marked by the scheduling of the next one.

NDI has found that gatherings that center around fresh thinking take on an entirely different structure and tone. Along with occasionally having conventional meetings, we have an ever-evolving menu of get-togethers, including brainstorms, mindmaps, critiques, and group evaluations. Their site and size are continually varied, from full-staff concept jamborees to intimate, creative duets.

During these confabs, all opinions are considered equally valid, debate is discouraged, and every notion is written or (preferably) sketched out on paper or an electronic "blackboard." While there is a principal subject, staying on it is not necessarily required, since associative thinking is as valued as logically connected responses. Rather than the mere passing on of information and preformed opinion, the priority is to stimulate, tease out, and provoke ideas, as well as provide an audience for them.

The group at this particular rendezvous wasted no time demonizing the presumed enemy of creative design embodied by the threat of having to design a world car. Since NDI was invented to create distinctive cars, any concept that mandated a generic, undifferentiated identity was seen as dangerous to our very raison d'être. After a period of considerable whining about the issue, one design manager, Bruce Campbell, quietly reminded everyone that "despite our protests, and whether we like it or not, there are some very successful world cars out there."

Silence.

Glares.

The dragon had entered the room.

At this point I suggested, "This feels important. Let's go with it!"

Campbell persisted, urging the group to try to name them. The board quickly filled with famous car names like the Porsche 911, Volvo, Volkswagen Beetle, Jeep, Benz, and BMW. This list was surprisingly short and easy to agree upon.

More silence.

Uneasy shifting.

Palpable dragon's breath.

Then, suddenly, twenty-some people simultaneously saw the same pattern on the blackboard. None of the cars noted was bland and, more amazingly, none had been conceived as a world car. Indeed, perhaps most surprising of all, each of these globally successful cars had been designed for a highly specified, limited niche market, and one had been commissioned by the Führer to be restricted for sale to only his people—the Volkswagen!

The planners who had conceived this assignment assumed that a world car, one whose appeal had to cross all cultural boundaries, would have to be neutral. We had now realized that it was the very specificity and local authenticity of truly global design that lent it the sense of romantic, even exotic appeal to diverse cultures. Furthermore, these cars were compelling for unpredicted and sometimes ludicrously unintended reasons that varied from country to country. Certainly, Hitler would have been horrified to learn that his "people's car" would emerge in America throughout the sixties and beyond as a ubiquitous symbol of freedom and rebellion among college students.

With our new understanding that producing a global car would not mean designing one to appease the lowest common denominator, NDI was not only eager to accept the assignment but no longer threatened by what it represented. We had not simply debated the issue rooted to our initial position. We had embraced this dragon by going past our fears and the common understanding of the issue itself. Rather than dismissing it out of hand, we entered its domain and accepted its assumptions. We then looked back at our own domain and arrived at a new position outside both, one we might never have reached otherwise. The parent company received an enthusiastic report, but hardly for the reasons it expected. However, it had learned something new and significant.

What we had come to understand was that the view from the dragon's mouth offered a dramatic shift in perspective, revealing new angles, previously unseen patterns, and unimagined possibilities. While it is certainly beyond the scope of this book to delve into the strangely dual-faced nature of reality at the deepest levels of understanding, the list of such realizations has become quite familiar. Creativity operates like a joke. Genius approaches madness approaches genius. Light turns out to be both particle *and* wave. Space and time prove to be aspects of a space/time continuum. And now, although not on quite the same level of exalted revelation, world cars are revealed to have been conceived as niche vehicles.

Characteristic of such discoveries is the sense that the new truths were always there in plain sight but rendered invisible or menacing by an associated language and a stubborn set of assumptions. And in this case, the presumed draconian concept wound up supporting and strengthening the very position we thought it attacked.

***

The process of *embracing the dragon* is like a reversible chemical reaction; it works equally well in either direction. In other words, the potential for acquiring fresh insights is available whether one is the threatened, or the threatening, party. Ironically, the first time the full value of this principle became clear to me was at the very launching of NDI, when I, or at least an idea I had, seemed ominous to someone else—in this case, the president of Nissan, Takashi Ishihara.

Among my earliest assumptions about NDI was that it would have a group of engineers as an integral part of its design team. The last thing I wanted was for us to be limited to futuristic "show" vehicles, unrealistic car-toons that might hopefully influence Nissan's product line. The more accurate and thorough our designs, the greater their chance for ultimate realization. After all, we would be designing an enormously complex product for a parent company located halfway around the world. So I was utterly unprepared for Nissan's negative reaction to what I thought was a virtually self-evident requirement.

Mr. Ishihara, however, had envisioned a design satellite remote from headquarters precisely because of the conservative, repressive character of its engineering-dominant atmosphere. Here was an opportunity, he felt, for design to flourish away from a corporate culture that had stifled it for decades.

There is a long-standing tension between designers and engineers, not unlike the relationship between architects and builders. Engineers, it has been said, are concerned with making things work, designers with making them workable. Put another way, engineers labor in the realm between pure science and applied technology, designers between technology and its meaning to people. From the viewpoint of traditional engineers, designers are decorative artists with little grasp of what it takes to build a car or make it work. To the designers, engineers are technicians so lost in the parts and pieces they are blind to the expressive power of the fully integrated whole. Having studied mechanical engineering at Ohio State University before tackling design at a school of fine arts, however, I saw no necessary evil in what engineering represented to the process of design. Trouble maybe, but not evil.

Away from work, most engineers are as moved by the sensuous and aesthetic dimensions of an automobile as anyone else. At work, however, the overwhelmingly analytical, coolly objective nature of their approach tends to splinter apart and suppress this response. The car becomes a conglomeration of discrete elements whose manufacture, assembly, and performance are the engineers' heavy burden. Because I had been attracted to design in the first place by its unique marriage of the objective and the subjective, of both left and right brain activity as well as science and art, any forced division of this essentially bipolar nature was disturbing. If I had to sum up my principal motivation as a designer, it is to make what works beautiful and what's beautiful work. This could not be accomplished without the partnership of engineering and design.

But in most corporate battles at Nissan, the analytic, objective argument of engineering was prevailing over the more intuitive, artistic one of design, and Mr. Ishihara was becoming increasingly concerned with what was being lost. Although I understood his intention of protecting the designers, I was nonetheless surprised that *he* was surprised at my strong desire to have engineers as part of NDI's design team. Since our first president, Kazumi Yotsumoto, felt that this request would directly threaten one of the primary motivations behind Ishihara's dream, he wisely counseled me to make a full and formal presentation of the issue to him on the occasion of his first visit to San Diego in 1980. After all, he had gone to unprecedented and considerable lengths within his own culture to assure our creative freedom, and I had no desire to appear churlish at our first negotiation.

I needed to find a means of presenting the importance of engineers to the design process in a way that would diminish their apparent threat to it. As the dragon in this piece, I was beginning to engage with the apprehensions I was arousing in another person. And it was in thinking about how to explain a concept that to me seemed self-evident, to someone for whom it did not, that surprising realizations began to surface. But I first had to step into his very foreign shoes.

As we did not yet have our building, we met in a hotel suite on an atypically humid day in San Diego. Ishihara was a plain-spoken, pugnacious man, and it was easy to imagine the full weight of Nissan resting easily on his sturdy frame. Yet, I recall being surprised every time we met at how slight he actually was. I proceeded to explain why engineering was an integral and vital part of the design process itself, and how nothing at Nissan could change significantly until engineering and design were brought even closer together. I told him about the dangers of overprotecting the designers from vitally needed information, and about the stimulation provided by the "obstacles" of manufacturing and the realities of basic physics.

As I droned on, he appeared to doze off in all the hot air. I hesitated momentarily, my eyes asking Mr. Yotsumoto, "What now?" He smiled and nodded for me to continue, and I now felt as ridiculous as when observed delivering a passionate speech, while driving, to that equally inert and transparently indifferent audience, the car windshield.

The instant I concluded my presentation, Mr. Ishihara's eyes abruptly opened. He cut directly to his area of greatest concern. "But why would you want the enemy with you?"

"They're *not* the enemy," I replied with renewed vigor, seeing he was considerably more responsive (and far less transparent) than my windshield. "And even if they were," I continued, suddenly seeing the way, "*with* us is exactly where we'd want them!"

Ishihara sat up and became more animated. "But we have hundreds of engineers—we *are* engineers!" he proclaimed.

"We don't want redundant engineering, though. You're quite right about that," I responded. "We have to develop and utilize a unique kind of engineering. What we need are not production engineers, but engineers of the concept, engineers whose responsibility it would be to find a hundred ways we might be able to do something new rather than a thousand reasons why we couldn't."

For Ishihara, it was becoming apparent that engineering was not necessarily antithetical to creative design, and that it would even serve at times as a stimulus for new thinking. For me, having to articulate this apparently threatening issue from his point of view gave me far greater understanding about the character of the engineers we would want to look for and the distinctly conceptual nature of our proposed engineering department. Neither of us left this exchange with our initially polarized positions intact. They had each been expanded to incorporate aspects of the opposing point of view, and had transmuted into forms we had not previously perceived.

He agreed to our request, as well as to an additional request for a Japanese liaison engineer familiar with Nissan's methodology to be fully integrated into the NDI engineering team. The result of this arrangement, to the continuing delight of the parent company, has been the consistent delivery of innovative design concepts that are more than ninety-five percent production-ready. Meaning, less than five percent of each design has needed to change during the final manufacturing development phase. This has not only proved to be a highly efficient process, it has also resulted in end products that are remarkably close to the initial concepts. The situation is a far cry from the nearly unrecognizable distant cousins to the original ideas that used to roll off the production lines of GM, where the engineers and designers weren't separated by geographic, language, or cultural barriers. Or at least ones of which they were then aware.

Although there are still rifts and rough spots in the engineering/design relationship, the antipathy between the departments has been significantly reduced. Nissan's engineers continue to work with their time-honored methodologies. And for good reason. They work. The level of mechanical excellence of the company's products is undeniable. Corporations and departments work hard to support and defend their established procedures and fundamental principles. Building on them constitutes the bulk of their everyday worklives. Software, hardware, technical jargon, and methodologies grow naturally around them, providing focus and meaning to their work. It is not easy to genuinely consider an unfamiliar or unsettling position which, if acknowledged, would seem to deny the validity of what had been thought of as "normal" productive work, even if it could be helpful.

✳ ✳ ✳

There is clearly a similarity between *embracing the dragon* and *creative abrasion*. Both are strategies that utilize aspects of human interaction in organizations typically deemed negative, even hostile to productive work, for the purpose of stimulating creative thought. Furthermore, both aim at increasing tolerance for polarity, opposition, and ambiguity. While the differences between them are subtle, they are nonetheless important to clarify.

Creative abrasion is essentially an interpersonal process. It is a means for harnessing the frictional energies released between distinct perspectives and workstyles to generate new directions and novel solutions.

Embracing the dragon, on the other hand, is an intrapersonal measure. It is energized by a willingness to adopt an alien, even threatening viewpoint to gain a fresh, re-orienting take on an entrenched position. This process is specifically involved with "the other hand," as opposed to the interaction between two of them.

Yet another shared characteristic of these two vital strategies is the threat of disruption they represent to things as they are.

While discoveries that grow out of entertaining polar viewpoints can be revelatory and profitable, it is instinctive human nature to avoid "the other side." Every business needs to develop strategies to overcome the fear, discomfort, and resistance. Fostering a corporate atmosphere that accommodates the opposing point of view without negative repercussions is a good starting point, but even this is not easy. While a CEO can announce to a staff that dissenting opinions are welcome at any time, there remains a reluctance to openly state them. The fear factor looms large in corporate life, and going against the tide is never readily acceptable.

Potentially valuable ideas that might otherwise provide healthy counterpoint often become exaggerated, politicized, and rendered ominous by their frequent association with a competing company, discipline, or department. At Nissan, such a situation existed between engineering and design, and any benefit or opportunity for divergent thinking between them was lost, hidden from view by the mantra of familiar, mutually critical rhetoric.

Furthermore, there is a certain sense of stability and security in labeling and maintaining the opposition as "the enemy." Groups often define themselves by what they stand *against*, which can feel like a protective and unifying bond with armor of its own language and code of identity. Yet, in an important sense, the questions and doubts surrounding an existing point of view belong to it every bit as much as the supporting evidence and benefits deriving from it. By shifting from a closed to an open stance towards the very forces that have been perceived (and sometimes even shown themselves) to be hostile, some surprising and very real opportunities can arise. More often than not, breakthroughs occur precisely when positions toward which we have great antipathy are not only considered, but openly embraced.

∗∗∗

At NDI we still enter with trepidation into something we fear might engulf us, but upon stepping past the threshold, often find our perceptions immediately transformed.

"I wonder if I shall fall right through the earth!" asked Lewis Carroll's Alice after plummeting into the infamous hole leading to

Wonderland. "How funny it'll seem to come out among the people that walk with their head downwards! The Antipathies, I think—!"[1]

The dragon that had led Alice through to "the other side" and transformed her (and our) perception forever, was nothing more threatening than a rabbit.

PART II

Unprecedented Thinking

To live into the future means to leap into the unknown, and this requires a degree of courage for which there is no immediate precedent and which few people realize.

Rollo May[1]

But there are no such things as future events. They can't be known until they happen.

Charles Hartsborne[2]

4

Creative Questions Before Creative Answers

We all leapt at the opportunity to design a line of preschool day-care furniture for the Angeles Group of Saint Louis, one of the world's premier manufacturers. This was as great a stretch for a team of automobile designers as we could imagine, but immediately appealing to a crew that grasped the connection between imagination and childhood.

The assignment included a line of tables, bookshelves, cubbies, and eventually even tricycles; but we began with one of the classic design challenges: the chair. The boards filled quickly with all manner of ingenious concepts. While they were stable, practical, ergonomically correct, and buildable, however, they lacked something vital we couldn't quite identify. Good design both visually expresses the nature of a product's use and intimates something about the character of its users. But for anyone looking at these sketches who was unaware of the miniaturized scale, there was nothing in the proportions of the design or the relationships of the parts that suggested they were intended for children. The concepts all stubbornly remained little adult chairs.

One of the designers, Diane Allen, peopled all her sketches with deftly drawn, wonderfully whimsical images of kids. While scanning over them at a review session one afternoon, we all marveled at how perfectly she'd captured "child-ness." And the drawings were not merely generically childlike. They precisely nailed those universally endearing qualities of squat, chunky, determined, yet wholly dependent awkwardness that exists fleetingly between the ages of three and five years. Although we wanted to avoid cuteness or toylike-ness in our designs, even Diane hadn't yet found the right spirit in her chairs.

And so, as we puzzled over the sketches, I was moved to utter one of those apparently dumb questions that sometimes leap to the mind when dealing with an imponderable.

"What's a kid?" I asked.

"A little adult," was the general response.

"No," piped up someone from the midst of the group. "A kid's a *misshapen* adult!"

We all laughed, but here was the vital distinction we needed to differentiate between a little adult chair and one with the soul of a preschooler. This was what Diane had caught in her drawings. A child at this stage is all torso and head, with chubby little undifferentiated arms and legs—all out of proportion! Within days, we had a virtual schoolroom filled with possibilities. The chair finally selected for production had a smallish seat connected by spherical "joints" to thick, tubular legs wearing rubbery "socks" to prevent scuffing. It was sturdy, built low to the ground, and had just the kind of clumsy yet purposeful appeal we were looking for. When children in Asia and Europe as well as America finally saw the manufactured chairs, they ran to them like newly found old friends.

The critical question, "What's a kid," while central to the project, hadn't come up because it seemed so utterly unnecessary and obvious—something only an extraterrestrial might ask. But fundamental questions like these are vital because they can distance us from a subject. In the context, this one asked: How would you describe a preschooler to someone who had never seen one? Furthermore, it forced us to use our eyes to freshly perceive what was *there*, rather than work only with what we knew to be a child in the dictionary sense, or what a child is relative to an adult.

*** * ***

For an automobile manufacturing company the most penetrating (and to many, the most disturbing) question in the midst of business-as-usual can be: What is a car? *Creative questions* are not necessarily complex. Nor do they have to deal with exotic, unknown regions. They are often disarmingly simple, and force a reconsideration of areas considered known and familiar. Such questions are particularly effective in jarring "the known" loose from its all-too-familiar moorings. If asked at the right times, they are also helpful in clearing away the thick, dead underbrush of old associations and assumptions, allowing for fresh light on a subject. And the potential for the growth of new ideas.

The form of a question itself contains both the limits and the potential character of its possible answers. Thinking about a car as a people-mover suggests an utterly different set of possibilities than framing it as a mode of personal transportation, an expression of individual style, or a mobile pollution device on four wheels. Companies that value idea-making need to expend considerable energy on reframing (or unframing) issues before resolving them.

*** * ***

Once we had completed the forms and concepts for the chairs, tables, bookcases, and cubbies, the Angeles people asked NDI to come up with a family of appropriate colors for the line. "Appropriate" was the key word here, and the question was how to determine which shades would be appealing to a group of three- to five-year-olds. Certainly, conventional focus groups or marketing surveys would be ineffective in this case.

Since NDI typically likes to observe people and the products being designed for them interacting in situ, the staff began visiting daycare centers, watching, getting into the spirit. Brenda Parkin, the head of NDI's Color Studio, was wandering around in the happy tumult of one of the classrooms when she had a sudden insight. Crouching beside a child, she asked if she might borrow his box of crayons.

Realizing what Ms. Parkin was on to, the designers quickly began examining everyone's boxes of Crayolas, noting which crayons were the shortest and therefore the most often used. Here was a surefire approach to learning which colors were alive to children. To the designer's surprise, they were *not* the primary, party-balloon colors most often associated with children, but rather the subtlest, most nuanced, most "adult" tones; the mauves, pale greens, and complex shades of gray; the colors of wind and thunder, of shadows and hugs, and of imaginary worlds seen with eyes at the height of their powers and sensitivity. NDI had found the answers to the client's request, but only after first finding an innovative way of asking the question. There was more in a box of Crayolas, as it turned out, than crayons.

***

During the course of a project, I enjoy wandering around the studios, as much to stimulate my own thinking as to check on the progress of the work. Sometimes, when I ask how things are going, I encounter such phrases as "I'm lost," "I'm drawing a blank," or "I have absolutely no idea." I have learned to feel encouraged by such responses that some innovative thinking is imminent. "Drawing a blank" suggests just the kind of clean slate on which the mind can configure a fresh image. And a state of "having no idea" often precedes the conception of a new one. The managers are urged to remain unconcerned upon observing an apparently lost staff, as they may well be lost in thought, not a bad place to be.

Designers are notoriously quick at drawing their pencils and firing away at solutions. When confronted with a situation for which there is no immediately obvious answer, there is a great temptation for any professional to move too quickly into a problem-solving mode, which is quite distinct from the less concrete business of creative ideation. Early answers provide an immediate sense of security and relief from the very real discomfort and anxiety posed by tough questions. Because they alleviate the uneasy, even threatening feeling that inevitably accompanies a state of not-knowing, such answers quickly become precious to us—too precious—and amount to preconceptions, which are one of the great impediments to spontaneous thinking.

Resisting the temptation to jump to quick solutions (*or* obvious questions) is vital, and our most creative people seem to be able to tolerate working in a state of limbo. Often, they even court it.

Remaining "of two minds" about a topic and staying with the ambiguity is essential for innovative thinking. David Bohm, the noted Cambridge physicist/philosopher, says that "staying with [ambivalence] gives a creator access to great energy and insight into nuances usually obscured by our polarized patterns of thought."[1]

Groups exhibit the same anxiety and overeagerness for quick solutions as individuals do, and tend to be quite skilled at moving into problem-solving modes. But prolonging the time a group remains in a state of ambiguity by urging creative questioning requires some counterintuitive strategies for leadership.

We were recently struggling to formulate a direction for the next Sentra, an entry-level vehicle deemed practical, efficient, and reasonably priced, a reliable product with all the character and excitement of—something reliable. Upon talking with current owners, we found little pride or passion for their cars. "It never lets me down, but it's just not *me!*" said one defensively. Long considered a stepping-stone product, it was used to bring young buyers into the corporate lineup with the hope of then moving them up to higher-bracket cars. This understanding of the Sentra could hardly have been expected to inspire memorable design.

Clearly, the car needed to find its own character, its "Sentra-ness." At a loss as to which direction to take it, the designers needed a verbal compass-setting for their creative efforts, so they met again with members of the Design Context Lab who had been studying the current car, its users, and principal competition. As the discussion ambled around the issue (meandering, apparently pointless conversations can be quite useful when mapping out unfamiliar terrain), one designer suggested that the problem was that the Sentra had always emulated the car at the top of its class, the Maxima, a car with considerable "-ness." As a result, the design celebrated what the car was *not*. Why, continued another, couldn't we refocus the next design on the true character of the car itself, the Sentra as an end rather than a means to one? A destination product.

That question and that phrase, *destination product*, resonated for the group and stuck as a rallying cry throughout the project. It immediately prompted multiple images and new options. Feeling relief and considerable eagerness to get moving, I suggested we now zero in on some specific design directions.

"Wrrong!" intoned Nick Backlund, the Design Context Lab manager. "Let's *not* focus yet. Let's adjourn." He was one hundred percent right, and we did just that.

In my rush for an answer, I was about to close a window that had just been opened. Too many managers and executives see their primary roles as continually pushing for clarity and bottom-line resolution. They assume that to run or end a meeting without a clear direction is to fail. Noncommitment to a point of view is considered an equivocation, a position of weakness. In fact, it is a highly challenging and brave state of mind to retain, requiring a secure sense of self and an awareness that real confidence lies outside any specific ideological position. The limbo-space, that uncommitted, nonbiased, and uncomfortable region in between zones of familiar knowledge, is precisely where most of the potential for original thought exists.

NDI restricts its early brainstorming sessions to searching for *creative questions* as well as new ways of stating an assignment. We find it useful to halt the meetings just at the point the questions become provocative, when we can envision no clear route to a solution. Which means our leaders often find themselves in the novel position of *warding off* closure! In effect, Mr. Backlund pushed the "pause" rather than the "off" button, leaving everyone in a state of deliberate uncertainty and imbalance. Everyone was then encouraged *not to think about* the subject for a while.

By allowing mental time and space for the preconscious to join in the search, there was access to the further energies of associations, intuitions, unexplored connections, and synthesis. Which meant, beyond the linear, verbal, analytic work done in sorting and recognizing an issue, the staff was now fully motivated to provide the yearned-for balance and resolution, which will be the next Sentra (due for release in 1999).

The need to relieve anxiety by jumping to an early solution—almost *any* solution—has been reinforced by the answer-emphasis of our educational systems, both Eastern and Western. And the ability to ask good questions is not one that will be enhanced by the increased reliance on computers as educational tools. We're graded solely on our answers and further rewarded by the speed of achieving them. This is but one of the ways in which we unknowingly stifle creativity in students as well as adults in the workplace.

A fine way to judge whether a situation is likely to provoke original thinking is to assess the character of the questions arising. If they are erudite, firmly grounded, eloquent, and well considered, it is a good bet that there will be no new ideas. Such questions often serve more as challenges than genuine probes into unfamiliar terrain, and are meant to impress with the questioner's deep grasp of a subject. They cloak any actual sense of confusion or lack of answers. The Q&A sessions at most professional conferences are filled with these kinds of mini ad hoc speeches thinly disguised as questions. Something about the atmosphere or underlying purpose of such gatherings is inhibiting to the more spontaneous, less guarded queries—the "what ifs," "why nots," "couldn't we justs," and "I don't get its" that so deftly pop the cork and unleash the fizz. Such questions, however, risk revealing possible areas of ignorance or the lack of a clue about what to do next. They are unguarded, open requests for insight and direction, and they need the safety of a supportive atmosphere and some coaxing from sensitive leadership to emerge. It helps, for example, if the staff can say "wrong" to the boss without fear of reprisals.

Of course, there must eventually be an answer. And a good one is imminent once a pithy question has been achieved. We usually speak of answers as the ends and questions as the means. Prioritizing *creative questions over creative answers* suggests the inversion of this conventional and pervasive viewpoint.

***

Distinguishing between good questions and merely adequate ones is, of course, mandatory. And relatively easy. When Diane Allen first hired on as a car designer, she attracted considerable attention as a female in a male-dominated profession. I was at her side during one entertaining interview when a reporter asked, "What do you offer design as a woman, Diane?" After a considerable pause Diane turned to me and asked, "What do *you* bring to design as a man, Jerry?" I had never been asked that question and had no ready answer. Faces went blank, heads tilted, and the journalist's pen remained motionless over his pad. Diane's question in response to the reporter's predictable one was a stopper. With an honest, one-sentence query, she elevated the issue to a larger, deeper, and far more interesting plane: the relationship between gender and design.

Good questions are nearly always surprising, provocative, and seem to emanate from apparently skewed vantage points. However, not all original queries are incisive. The good ones are destabilizing. They have the effect of tipping the plane of a discussion, which may be why we tilt our heads upon hearing one! They open new routes to a subject, and often treat it as though it was being dealt with for the first time, returning to its underlying basics.

Sometimes, a timely question is *itself* the answer. One of the great joys of my time at General Motors was working under the late Jack Humbert, the chief designer of Pontiac, during a wonderful spell in the sixties. I'm still striving for the grace, wisdom, and ease of his almost invisible style of leadership. Pauline Kael, the great (and sorely missed) film critic for the *New Yorker*, once said that certain stars had an inner calm, what she termed a "quiet center," that lent them a powerful presence on the screen and a universal appeal. Jack had that.

One day, several of us at GM were puzzling over a rear fender configuration on the Grand Prix that looked abruptly truncated regardless of what we did to it. We sketched, gestured, and argued over how to visually lengthen it. We added horizontal lines, grooves, flattened the forms, and stretched them taut. Nothing worked. Jack sat nearby, amused by our earnest efforts. Eventually, he sauntered over, glanced at the offending fender, and asked quietly, "Why don't you just make it longer?" He walked off smiling, leaving us red-faced and wondering why, among several thousand suggested solutions, no one had thought to ask this simple question.

Ironically, however, creative solutions inevitably pose new problems. An innovative answer is therefore never a plateau or mental stopping point. In the deepest sense, the entire subject is elliptical and unending. A truly creative answer is, after all, nothing more (or less) than a new set of questions.

***

It is perhaps not surprising that when I was considering which anecdotes might best illuminate the prioritization of questions over answers, many of those that immediately occurred to me concerned the creation of products for children. Kids come into the world with no preconceptions or biases, save their powerful instincts for curiosity and questioning. They are blessed, therefore, with the ideal disposition to embrace and even *enjoy* ambiguity. Children spend their waking hours sniffing, tasting, looking, listening, touching, and trying things out, searching this way and that. And loving the process. Of course, they're delighted at finding answers. But not for long.

It's all about the quest. And the questions. Especially that one most universal, irritating, and difficult to answer of all—why.

Right?

5

Stepping Back from the Canvas

The staff was bogging down midway through the design of the Pathfinder. Concept sketches seemed tired variations on a familiar theme. The clay model in the platform remained a formless lump, stubbornly resisting our efforts to breathe life into it. And the ordinarily stimulating clutter and clatter of studio life had become a messy, noisy source of disorder and irritation. Tension was rising, solutions weren't coming, and the deadline was looming.

Rather than urging everyone to hunker down and increase the pressure, I impulsively got on the company pager and announced, "Movie time." We all gathered in the lobby, which had become our preferred general meeting place, to decide which film we should see. Picking one was half the fun, but this time it was an easy decision, since we had one that was clearly an "NDI film." And in the middle of the day, the entire company, including the shop, secretaries, and maintenance crew, went to see the opening of *The Silence of the Lambs.*

I had forgotten entirely about a phone interview scheduled for that afternoon, and had also neglected to instruct the temporary receptionist who stayed behind not to feel compelled to inform any callers as to exactly why no one was available. The next day a writer from *AutoWeek* magazine who had called during "hooky time" asked me if we had really closed NDI midday and gone to the movies. "Is this for the record?" I said. "Oh yes," he replied, "we'd like to understand the connection between serial murder and car design." Figuring we had been caught in the act, I said, "Well, I'm actually a bit surprised you don't know. You see, they're both about realizing fantasies, only perhaps ours are hopefully somewhat less destructive!"

Upon returning from the film, there was much chatter among the staff about how delicious it had been to leave a theater squinting guiltily into the midafternoon sun, knowing we had been "baad" together. As everyone returned to their work, conversation continued about the film (considered a winner, but not as creative as *Manhunter*). The tension in the building began to dissipate. Within days the ideas again started flowing, knotty problem areas unraveled, and the design began to lead the designers, a sure sign that a strong concept was emerging.

The germane issues here concerned the vital need to honor the push and pull of creative ideation, a rhythmic (though not regular) process. Rather than "amping up" the pressure when a staff is struggling, the *creative priority* often suggests a releasing of tension and a *stepping back* from the immediate problems as a far more effective managerial strategy. When ideas are required, the meaning and value of efficiency at all costs is placed in sharp contrast to the need for downtime, awaytime, and creative playtime, not at the conclusion of a project, but often in the midst of its most intense and stressful developmental phases.

Of course, it is not about the movies. It is about the disruption, the distraction, and the distancing. What is needed is an occasional, well-timed disengagement from the continually narrowing focus that necessarily accompanies the intense concentration of a creative search. Sometimes we will order in a bunch of pizzas, go to play beach volleyball, or bus ourselves to a local museum or gallery show. Whatever we do, it cannot be regular, expected, or often. And it has to be in the middle of a workday when we are breaking the rules as well as the routine, when things are stuck and behind schedule. That is when backing away works its magic.

Just before going to see *The Silence of the Lambs* I was asked by NDI's patient and perceptive new president at the time, Kengo Ishida, why we were leaving *then*, that day, when we were so far behind. Although he was in no way a typical Japanese "salaryman," he had not yet worked with us long enough to feel comfortable in such a dramatically different work atmosphere. He eventually developed an exquisite grasp of what we were doing and became a true partner (and close friend) in working out some of our critical strategies. But at that time, I fully understood his apprehension and deeply appreciated his tolerance for NDI's peculiar ways. "We're going now, Kengo-san, *because* we're behind."

The cost to Nissan for our truancy was fifty movie tickets, fifty bags of popcorn, and about fifty extra minutes of lunchtime. The payoff was a flood of ideas for an international product representing hundreds of millions of dollars in development investment.

❈ ❈ ❈

One of the most valuable lessons I took away from art school was the dire need to pull away from continual face-to-face involvement with a painting—to *step back from the canvas*. Physically as well as mentally. No second glances. "Just put everything down," my painting instructor would command when he saw me wrestling with a large canvas, "cap the tubes, soak your brushes, and get the hell away from here!"

Inevitably, after the rush of the initial strokes of paint on a canvas, everything seems to fall apart. The clarity, potency, and promise of the first bold gestures gradually reveal unexpected complexities and problem areas, tangles of seemingly unresolvable issues. Painter and painting become engaged in a heated, sometimes clumsy, yet vital dance of steps and missteps, actions and reactions, happy accidents and unhappy miscues. Persisting, working past the point of frustration, is of course vital to the process. But when the contrast between what is envisioned and what is emerging eventually becomes too great, that is the time to get away from hands-on, conscious involvement in the work.

Stopping midstream is not easy, immediately relieving, or even necessarily pleasant. Considerably more discipline is required to halt work than to keep at it while ambiguous directions nag for resolution. Walking away feels a lot like giving up at such moments. And that is precisely what's needed. Nothing can so effectively move work forward at times as *not working*.

It might at first seem odd to reference lessons discovered at an art school in a book on business management. Not that anyone there had any real interest in teaching business skills. But in the course of learning about such things as the importance of occasionally *stepping back* from intense involvement in work, I was inadvertently coming to terms with handling and managing critical aspects of the creative process. Leading and creating are intimately connected activities, both being involved with initiation, forward movement, and action at the edge of the known.

They are also both concerned with the mysteries of human motivation. But conventional styles of leadership are not always consistent with a group for whom idea-making is a priority. The instructors (all practicing artists and designers) at the Cleveland Institute of Art knew better than to try to externally motivate creativity. What they knew instinctively was how to get out of its way, how to get *behind* it.

Dealing with a faltering staff such as the one assigned the Pathfinder project is always a perplexing and stressful situation for organizations. Ordinarily strong groups with highly successful track records, effective methodologies, and a firm grasp of a project's importance can unaccountably lose all confidence for a time, become hopelessly lost, inept, a shambles. This was the prevailing mood of the Pathfinder group which, in such a state, were anything but finders of paths. There are any number of possible reasons, not always ready solutions.

Reducing the pressure, focus, and sense of urgency of a blocked group, however, runs counter to prevailing norms of safe and sound management. Leaders feel reassured seeing their people steadily, arduously toiling away, heads bent over desks, noses to the grindstone; and in tough times they want even more reassurance. In Japan, there is the further unstated obligation of continually working long hours, burning the midnight oil, whether it's productive or not.

Managers typically have three motivational strategies to get things moving when ideas are not flowing, ranging in effectiveness from harmless (but generally ineffective) to downright disastrous; pep talks, heightened competitiveness, and intimidation.

✳✳✳

Bill Mitchell, the vice president of Styling when I joined GM, was famous in the industry for his pep talks. He was a legendary figure in American automotive history; his authority was absolute and his influence and power throughout the corporation were formidable. If George Patton had had automotive design talent he could have slid into Mitchell's role without having to adjust his style. He was a blunt bulldog of a man, an ex-boxer who could by turns intimidate or inspire. He was simultaneously gregarious and insensitive, and the atmosphere around him was invariably entertaining, tense, and unpredictable.

But his enthusiasm and the level of confidence he had in his own intuition were infectious. When he was concerned about a flagging level of energy and direction in the studios, he'd gather everyone (well over a thousand people) in the vast Styling Dome for one of his legendary pep talks. Off-color metaphors flew, along with lots of car-racing and sports analogies. But they were delivered with such uninhibited passion and confidence that the entire assemblage was mesmerized and often inspired. It was like watching one of Hollywood's trite, manipulative summer blockbusters, a film you were embarrassed to say you enjoyed. He seemed able to rally and energize an entire army . . . occasionally.

Looking back now, I realize it was less the content of his talks that did the trick than the performances themselves. They offered a diverting break from the task, along with an infectious display of energy and zeal. Furthermore, they got everyone together and away from their work.

Pep talks do not necessarily stand in the way of a group reconstituting itself. Although they can be mildly irritating, especially when the staff is in a funk, a charismatic leader can sometimes restore direction and generate some enthusiasm.

More often than not, however, Mitchell and others at GM turned to intimidation, and most of the pep talks were little more than thinly veiled threats. Too many corporations attempt to motivate by an excessive reliance on competition and even fear. What might work for stimulating a sales force, military troops, or a basketball team does not work for encouraging imaginative thinking.

No one at General Motors ever questioned whether competition was an effective motivator for creative work. It was accepted as a universal and self-evident truth. Furthermore, the particular character of the corporation's competitive atmosphere struck me as especially bothersome; it was inward-looking and negative in tone. The Styling building perfectly mirrored the deeply ingrained organizational structure with its historic, built-in rivalry between its five (now seven) autonomous divisions. Many of them, after all, were larger by themselves than most other entire car companies, so most of the serious competition for any line of GM cars was thought to be another line of GM cars. And many high-level executives made their way up the ladder by bringing their own division to the top of the heap at the expense of another division. There was a resulting intramural quality to the competition, and designers representing the various car groups were encouraged to compete *against* each other rather than *for* the market. When the executives weren't happy with the creative output in a studio, they'd let us know what was happening "down the hall."

"Better watch out, Hirshberg," I was warned when I was chief designer of Pontiac, "those guys from Chevy are *hot*, and they're on the warpath!" Or later, when I was chief of Buick: "Olds studio is making you guys look bad." Of course, the impact on the creative process was exactly the opposite of what was desired.

Before these "motivational" visits, the staff was completely involved in its work, stimulated intrinsically by the struggles and joys of the creative process itself. Afterwards, all they could think about was slipping behind in some mythical race, and that their futures were in jeopardy. The idea of risking "iffy" paths at such moments was unthinkable. Not surprisingly, the ideas that grew from a culture characterizing work as a "race" or a "battle" perfectly mirrored the culture itself. Competition spawned the familiar, designs that had proven successful in the past. It became increasingly difficult to distinguish one generation of Buicks from another, or even Buicks from Oldsmobiles or Chevrolets. Fear of failure bred avoidance of risk, which resulted in a closing down of the creative process.

***

When Bruce Campbell was named chief designer of NDI's new Green Studio, his laid-back form of leadership—or to some, his seeming lack of one—was vaguely threatening to many on both sides of the Pacific who were used to a more assertive, take-charge style. The new studio was being established to deal with increasing demands from the American market for more suitable interior designs in its cars. The greenhouse (cabin) of an automobile contains its most complex, congested, and expensive real estate. Issues of comfort, safety, and control clamor for attention and space amid a cluster of heating, ventilating, and air-conditioning ducts, multimode audio and communication systems, thick tangles of electrical and fiber-optic cable, an ever-expanding array of electronic gadgets, and that single most vital (to Americans) element of late twentieth century automotive progress, the cup holder.

The Japanese were famously fastidious about every detail of the car interior, and were understandably apprehensive about the thoroughness and experience of NDI's all-too-green Green Studio. Even beyond the engineering and ergonomic complexities, there were the potential consequences of regulatory, insurance, and legal requirements that had to be dealt with faultlessly. Yet, to many, the newly appointed manager appeared remarkably calm in the face of all this. Too calm.

Campbell has the serene eyes of someone who has lived near the sea for a very long time, and knows how to sail it. He has, and he does. He occasionally wears socks, and he gathers his shoulder-length, sandy blond hair together with a rubber band, but usually only when he has to make a formal presentation in Japan. While not a native Californian, he exemplifies the stereotype: big, easy, unhurried, and independent.

He came to NDI from a product design background, knew instinctively how things were assembled and built, and was not intimidated by complexity. He had no prior experience in the politics of a mega-corporation and felt no sense of urgency about his group looking busy or productive. During the early months of its existence, it appeared as though nothing much was happening in the fledgling studio at all.

While it is easy to see the progress of a car's exterior form, it is nearly impossible for casual visitors to assess the state of an evolving interior design. In Campbell's studio hundreds of parts and pieces littered every corner: a seat prototype here; a door-panel emerging on a specially constructed frame there; mirrors, knobs, buttons, and handles everywhere; and a steering wheel mounted incongruously on a designer's desk, which seemed to be going nowhere. Other than the few shows when everything was painstakingly assembled for review, the only place the whole design congealed was in Campbell's mind and those of his designers, whom he trusted implicitly.

Leading such a task was clearly not for anyone needing continual visual reassurance of forward movement. Yet, Green Studio was flourishing. When finally assembled, the new interiors were remarkably complete, well integrated, and teeming with novelty.

Furthermore, young designers and modelers who had previously struggled to find their own "voices," began showing substantial growth and new levels of self-confidence. In Green Studio, they seemed to have found the space to find themselves.

The value and wisdom of Campbell's style of leadership, which grew naturally from his easygoing character, began to emerge over time. With so much complexity surrounding his task, he made no effort to surround *it*. Rather, he immersed himself calmly in the middle of it, much in the manner he navigated his sleek little catamaran through tricky winds and shifting currents; sensing, monitoring, adjusting, aiding, and mostly following the flow.

To most, a leader is someone who goes out front, charts the course, and induces others to follow. It's the "charting the course" part that breaks down when leading for the *creative priority*. Original ideas establish their own directions, and realizing their potential means following their lead—not something traditional leaders do easily.

Yet another lesson inadvertently learned while at art school was that the means by which individuals access their imaginations are as astonishingly diverse as are the ideas themselves. The writer Patricia Hampl said in her eloquent piece, "The Lax Habits of the Free Imagination" in *The New York Times Book Review*,[1] that the creative individual is like "a good host attempting to draw out a shy guest." She further quoted Henry James, who referred to his genius as "mon bon," and said, ". . . let me fumble it gently and patiently out." Shy guests and pals don't respond well to bullying.

Instead of insisting on any preconceived approach, Bruce Campbell's focus was on ascertaining, accommodating, and supporting the wide variety of workstyles he found emerging around him. Individuals were free to grope for their own access codes leading to creative flow, and knew the boss was eager to support their search.

Some imaginations are ignited in the crossfire and collision of contrasting ideas in a bustling, crowded atmosphere. These people like to socialize, hopping from desk to desk, studio to studio to see what is happening elsewhere. They thrive on the light that sparks off abrading perspectives. Music, chatter, and "worksounds" provide the active ambiance preferred by this creative disposition.

For others, all such activity amounts to so much distraction and noise. A quiet, serene place is preferred, perhaps even utter solitude, an underrated and important component of imaginative thinking. Here, the roiling, competing precepts and concepts within have the stillness and sense of space in which to emerge. Going for a walk or drive, sitting alone in the library or other out-of-the-way space, or just being left alone to gaze out the window, daydreaming, are potent triggers for ideation.

For still others, intimate one-on-one dialogues are best. The give and take, push and pull, point and counterpoint of mutually shared ideas amounts to a creative duet. Two temporarily joined but differently voiced instruments of thought spin out unexpected turns and new tunes.

Making matters even more complicated for Campbell was that many of his people were stimulated by *all* these modes, but at different times, for different kinds of tasks and at different stages of a project. Taking an entire group to the movies or otherwise inducing it to *step back from the canvas* works best when there is a general malaise, a widespread feeling that the creative muse has been lost or blocked. More often, however, individuals within the group progress at their own rates, experiencing the ebb and flow of idea-formation with highly distinctive rhythm and tone.

Campbell was able to resist quick-scan assessments of this richly variegated work environment. This did not mean he was indecisive, fuzzy-minded, or the least bit "new-agey." But he did not assume that the "interactors" were just partying, the solitary daydreamers disengaged or lazy, or the isolated pairs merely gossiping. Although he was very clear about the assignments, the scheduling requirements, and his expectations, he intuitively grasped that leading the creative process called for the accommodation of a broad spectrum of approaches and behaviors. Furthermore, this level of trust and tolerance had to exist between staff members as well, who needed occasional encouragement from him to avoid comparative judgments about who seemed to be carrying their weight and who did not.

The experience of Green Studio helped us to understand that leading for creativity meant following the creative lead.

***

Classic "eureka" moments are perhaps the ultimate sense in life of receiving something for nothing, of being "in the zone." But arriving at these moments remains an elusive, deeply personal affair. At the moment of recognition, there seems to be a direct connection between brain and lungs, as though something fresh and lighter than air has been caught on a breath. Inhaled. Which is probably why our immediate reaction is inevitably a quick exhalation, a "hey" or "hah" or "aha."

The writer Robert Grudin said in his wonderful book on creativity and innovation that the word "inspiration" originally referred to a "breath of divinity or transfusion of soul from the gods," and today "denotes the experience of sudden insight that cuts across categories or otherwise leaps over normal steps of reasoning."[2] I cannot say I feel touched by religious divinity at these moments, but it is an undeniably uplifting experience of exquisite purity. And divine is precisely how it feels.

Once experienced, this fleeting yet powerfully gratifying whiff of fresh clarity becomes the object of a deep human craving. And since most people, at some level, have had innovative notions from time to time, it is safe to assume that there exists a widespread and intrinsic drive to create.

At the same time, monitoring and appropriately responding to the myriad ways individuals in any group prefer being approached, being included, or being led in their search, can be a daunting prospect. It will always be tempting for management to press for unanimity, which looks more purposeful and feels safer than relying on an internal, individual, and invisible drive.

If managing such a complex task while maintaining some semblance of optimism and order sounds intimidating or confusing— sleep on it! If it helps, take in a flick on failed transsexual serial killers.

Things will be clearer in the morning.

6

Failure, Cheating, and Play

Saturday mornings, carrying a snack and my tattered clarinet case, I eagerly took the bus to the University Circle area. Exiting at Severance Hall, the stately home of the Cleveland Orchestra, I wound my way through the leafy, park-like gardens of the Museum of Art, past the Institute of Art where I would one day study, and arrived at the Institute of Music ready for rehearsals. Although most of us were still in junior high school, there were some incredibly gifted kids in the Young People's Symphony Orchestra, and we played from real scores of the masterworks, pieces by Dvořák, Mozart, Liszt, and others.

We would occasionally have guest conductors, and certainly the most memorable experience I had there was playing under the baton of Leopold Stokowski, who spent a week with the orchestra preparing us for a concert featuring the Dvořák Ninth Symphony. Strictly speaking, I really didn't play under his baton, since he didn't use one. Didn't have to. With pointy, hawklike features topped by a crest of wild, white hair (I used to wonder if there wasn't some mysterious connection between pearly white hair and the physical act of conducting great music), he simply willed the music out of us. He seemed to treat this youthful ensemble with the same unsmiling intensity and occasional ferocity as I imagined he did the Philadelphia Orchestra. We liked that.

But we all dreaded his abrupt stops, when he would ask someone to play alone in order to work out some faulty intonation or awkward phrasing. Often, however, he stopped us when he heard something special in what an individual was doing with a particular passage, simply wanting everyone to hear the possibilities. Sometimes it was a remarkably subtle, barely perceivable hesitation or unexpected emphasis that transformed what at first seemed like nothing more than a connecting section of music into a moment of expressive significance itself.

When we all resumed playing the same part again, we each experimented with our own versions of what we had just heard. The results were amazing. We were breathing life and character into the music.

After the concert everyone marveled at how Stokowski had induced sounds from our instruments we didn't know were in them. In fact, much of what we were doing came from simply learning to listen to one another and then doing something of our own with what we heard.

We had been encouraged to freely use one another's ideas by one of the world's greatest conductors. When he once asked me to play a brief passage on the clarinet myself, I wasn't at first aware of what I was doing that had caught his attention. But when it was heard in a different and larger context, it evidently proved useful to the other musicians. Listening to the orchestra play through that same passage again, this time informed with the influence of my own phrasing, I began to really *hear* and understand my own natural "voice" at a deeper and more conscious level.

***

Yet another time music provided potent glimpses into the management of creative interaction was when I became, for a brief but exciting period, Jerry Paul, rock star. I had formed a little band while in college to earn extra money by playing at parties and dances. I sang lead and played bass guitar with a group that included my brother Bert, who *really* played guitar, and some musical friends. Although at first we did mostly covers, we slowly began developing our own sound, and I began writing songs.

Through friends of friends we eventually got an audition tape heard by people in the business, and three of these pieces were ultimately published, recorded, and released as singles nationally. A couple of managers took me on and, in spite of Art Garfunkel having retained his real name at around the same time, quickly changed mine to Jerry Paul (Paul is my middle name). "Hirshberg" evidently did not have the same ring as "Garfunkel."

One of the records, "Sparkling Blue," got an increasing amount of airtime and started showing up on Top 40 lists around the country. I began touring, leaving Ohio State during the weekends by small plane or bus to play at record hops, concerts, and radio and television appearances on all the local Bandstand-style shows at the time, learning about the rigors, thrills, and horrors of performing on the road. At the "height" of my rock career, I was occasionally used as an opening act for the likes of Bobby Rydell, Fabian, Frankie Avalon, and other lesser luminaries. These were particularly exciting gigs since there would generally be a dozen cops lined up in front of the stage, arms crossed, to protect the superstars from their rapacious fans. I found that nothing ever again made me feel quite so potent as performing while flanked by an armed guard. Even if they weren't really for me.

There were other times I felt somewhat less potent. At a nighttime performance outdoors in Buffalo, New York, during which I felt a real rapport with the sizable crowd in attendance, a light drizzle began to fall. The shafts of light from the spots became very dramatic in the clouds of mist (this was long before stage smoke became obligatory) and no one moved to leave. There was a rhythmic clapping and swaying to the beat, and I sidled forward to the microphone to belt out one last reprise. As I grabbed it, the shock sent me hurtling halfway across the stage. To my surprise, the clapping never stopped and everyone evidently thought I'd invented some hair-raising new move. You can get away with some amazing things at a rock concert.

"[The song] has a disarming folk-like feel. Paul sings of the joys of spending a lifetime with his gal. Happy take (industry-speak for a performance on tape that was a keeper—a winner) can happen," said the review of the record in *Cash Box*,[1] which gave it a Best Bet recommendation. Along with *Variety*, *Cash Box* was the music industry's trade journal. This article, along with a few aging 45 rpm records, a box of fan mail, a folder filled with hopeful, smiling pictures from the "Miss Sparkling Blue" competition, and most cherishable of all, some authentic jukebox tabs, are all that remain of the entire experience. Still, I did receive my last check in 1981 for $2.84 from BMI, which means the records were played as oldies-but-goodies at least seventy-one times somewhere in America that year.

Since I was still in my teens, nothing was more fantastic than driving around with my girlfriend-for-life-at-the-time and hearing the DJ suddenly sing out from the car radio, ". . . and now, from the WHK Fabulous 50 Official Tunedex, heerre's number seventeen, Jerry Paul and "sssSparkling Blue." Along with the police-protection performances and those times when the band and the crowd fused into one, these moments were surely my all-time personal pinnacles of cool.

Aside from quickly becoming disillusioned with the rock business in the early sixties, with its obligatory tours, crackerjack DJs, payola, five thousand screaming toughs at drafty stadiums and cavernous roller rinks, and awkward, lip-synched performances for TV gigs, I did have some truly meaningful experiences. Many of these were at the practice sessions and in the recording studios.

Fashioning a sound and improvising with the band long into the night, I learned once again about the joys of stealing good ideas, of jumping all over some entirely serendipitous passage, hearing intriguing possibilities in someone else's mistake, doing something of my own with it, and then folding it back into the evolving sound. And there was the equivalent pleasure of hearing something *I* was doing suddenly picked up, reframed, and incorporated into the mix. The music we were making with all this improvising/influencing was filled with experimentation, and was not very appealing to the ear. But when it all finally gelled, when every voice and instrument had found its place and purpose, the tight, locked-in togetherness was instantly audible to all. At these moments, the music seemed driven forward by its own internal engine, and we would all break into spontaneous and irrepressible laughter, driving the recording engineers crazy.

Creative music-making in a group incorporates the three principal elements of this chapter; picking up someone else's ideas, perceiving possibilities in the failed attempts, and playing around with them. In this context, of course, the specific meanings of "failure," "cheating," and "play" are freed of some of their usual connotations in a traditional work setting or educational institution.

They might at first appear to be an odd grouping. After all, the only commonly shared connection among them was that as kids we cheated in order to avoid failure and played around to avoid both. Certainly our most indelible memories of each of them as young students in the classroom were all negative, a terrible trio of actions held in universal contempt. Cheating was disallowed, failing was unacceptable, and playing around was something done outside class and after work was completed. Within the context of the school system and its traditional priorities (among which creative thinking is not highly placed), this made eminently good sense. But in uncritically characterizing them as no-no's when it comes to serious thinking or work, we have missed some extraordinarily useful and even vital dimensions they offer to the process of imaginative thought.

When I originally set out to write about these three elements of the *creative priority*, they were to have occupied three distinct chapters. But as I began to gather my thoughts, it became increasingly difficult to examine any of them for long without one or both of the others coming into play.

What we were doing in the recording studio involved a moment-by-moment alertness and mutual responsiveness to the potential that lurked in everything happening around us. Listening to each other and freely using what we heard was required, and the consequences of not doing so instantly audible to all. Of course, credit for a "stolen" inspiration was mandatory. The sax player winked at the guitarist who leaned into the bassist who smiled at the drummer for an inspired riff. What mattered was the quality of music being produced.

* * *

Munching on a sandwich while meandering around the NDI studios one lunchtime, I spotted an intriguing page poking out from a pile of drawings on the desk of Doug Wilson. He generated reams of such sheets, widely referred to as "Doug's doodles," each filled with concepts for assorted cars, car parts, and anything else that happened to flit across his mind. Whereas others enjoyed fleshing out an idea or refining it, it was this boundless conceptualizing that most turned him on. So his desk was always a fertile field for grazing. The particular page, which was upside-down when it first caught my attention, was filled with drawings for a now-defunct car called the Pulsar NX.

My eye went right to the upper rear quadrant of the car (that area including the rear window and trunk lid), which had been graphically set off by an unusually thick black line. This line interacted with other lines delineating the doors and side-window openings in such a manner that the entire vehicle seemed a set of cleverly interlocking panels all fitted together, with nothing extraneous, like a fully resolved, three-dimensional puzzle.

I drew a circle around the sketch and wrote the words "eureka" and "see me" on it. Racing back to my desk with Doug's "stolen" doodle in my mind, I began playing around with the myriad ideas it suggested. Since I perceived his design as having been sort of puzzled together, I could easily imagine it as an assortment of pieces that could be disassembled and refitted, a car with removable, replaceable panels for diverse uses. By altering just a few lines in the upper rear quadrant, it was possible to transform it from a little sport coupe to a two-door minivan. Wilson, I felt, was really on to something.

As everyone returned from lunch, I gathered them around his desk and displayed both his doodle and my hastily sketched derivations from it. There was an immediate wave of interest, and by the end of the day, a full-blown effort had commenced. The engineers began studying possible problems in such areas as hinges, structural reinforcements, and sealing. Some modelers and designers began mocking up a full-sized cardboard "van module." Others continued expanding the concept, creating a kind of hybrid car/truck by leaving the rear quadrant completely open.

What we were in the process of creating was a vehicle destined to become the world's first mass-manufactured modular automobile, a chameleon car whose owners could themselves convert it from a conventional coupe to a two-door minivan (later labeled the Sportbak version), to a useful little truck for hauling light loads, three cars in one.

To this day I have no idea if Doug Wilson consciously knew what his sketch was intimating or if I simply misread and imposed my own agenda on it. Even when I later asked him directly, he honestly didn't know if it was the functional dimensions of modularity that were on his mind or if he just liked the way it looked. It was a moot point, and didn't matter at all to Wilson, who was amused by all the fireworks his half-finished little drawing had ignited. The fact is, an idea was born in an atmosphere that did not frown on looking over someone else's work and taking inspiration from it.

Doug's doodles and Pulsar NX, world's first production modular car

At General Motors, each studio was secured from all the rest. Locks with secret codes were on each of the entrance doors and the worlds of Pontiac and Oldsmobile were sealed off from each other, with great solemnity, as well as from those of Cadillac, Chevrolet, or Buick. This was done to assure maximum differentiation between the divisions, and to honor and heighten the spirit of competition between them.

The arrangement accomplished several objectives. It did indeed provoke competition between the studios. It also increased the sense of intimidation and secrecy in the building. Rather than the fertile ambiance of a research lab or a creative design department, walking the dark, patrolled halls of the Styling building brought to mind the feeling of rigid compartmentalization of such institutions as the FBI or CIA—not referring here to those same initials on my aging sweatshirt from the Cleveland Institute of Art.

What the arrangement failed to accomplish, however, was its principal objective: maximum design differentiation between the corporation's divisions. Nor did it take advantage of the level of inspiration readily available among its considerable collection of talent.

Even within individual studios, this cordoned-off spirit between workers prevailed. There was the sense at the time that careers were at stake and that it was necessary to protect your ideas to gain credit for them in a crowded and highly competitive atmosphere. We all proceeded in the same cautious spirit that prevailed while taking tests in school, wrapping one arm around our work to block any errant glances. Eyes down. Closed off.

Of course, GM was hardly alone in fostering autonomous, self-subsistent work. Most workplaces, educational institutions, and organizations teach us to protect the authorship of our output at all costs. Understandably, there is a desire for acknowledgment and appreciation. Furthermore, as observed in Chapter 5, working in solitude can be invaluable. But there is also a great cost in suppressing the kind of ferment and stimulation that can occur naturally in a more open, correlative environment. Reading the developmental histories of many great ideas reveals considerably more ad hoc partnerships and mutually stimulating interactions among the supposedly solitary geniuses than was previously believed, even when they regarded each other as fierce competitors.

***

When incoming employees are told that "cheating" is encouraged at NDI, their initial apprehensions and expectations are transformed. A gathering of talented, competitive individuals is coaxed toward becoming a team of potentially creative collaborators who can inspire, or be inspired by, one another's work. There are no departmentally encoded locks, and the designers are encouraged to freely roam the studios and forage through the concepts, notes, and sketches of their colleagues. They may use any ideas that turn them on as long as they give them their own spin and acknowledge the inspiration. They are further told that their work will be used by others in the same way.

Significantly, even though there is continual movement between the studios and departments, there has been no problem in maintaining differentiation between the various designs being developed. Even when designers assigned to one project are told their thoughts are welcome at any time on a vehicle emerging next door, the diverse identities are distinctively honored. Awareness, exposure, and trust appear to lead to a greater, not a more homogenized, level of differentiated thinking.

Often, an abandoned path is picked up and followed by someone else who senses further potential in it. Other times, a sketch is "misread" or an idea interpreted as something far more interesting than the initial notion, and the resulting concept is completely surprising to its originator, who might then be motivated to reengage with it. It is not uncommon to see designers using someone else's idea that had failed in one context but seems to hold great promise in another. Unfinished, half-finished, discarded, and even failed directions take on new significance in such a culture.

Unfortunately, most people quickly discard their mistakes and hide the process by which they move forward in their work. This is not surprising, since *avoiding failure* and *protecting your ass* are perhaps the most universal of the unspoken organizational mandates.

Most work environments prefer a methodology and atmosphere more in line with the kind of virtual thinking done by a computer; sequential logic pursued along prescribed paths in a tidy, tight process disallowing error. Human brains, on the other hand, have wonderfully unique advantages over computer "brains" by being able to go beyond simple logic and to learn from their mistakes. While problem-solving can benefit from linear, step-by-step analysis, idea-formation benefits from the further use of blind alleys, flat-out errors, and happy accidents. Indeed, it was through our mistakes that we learned to learn in the first place.

Recently, a group of well-known artists, architects, designers, filmmakers, and others were asked to name the implement most essential for their work. The answers, along with the tools themselves, were included in an exhibit in New York called the Worklife Tools Exhibition. In response, I selected the kneaded eraser, which becomes my forgiving friend over the course of a project. While it starts life as a clean, gray, rectangular object, it gradually becomes molded into an amorphous shape, assumes my body temperature, and absorbs my mistakes and miscues as I worry a design into existence. But unlike the computer, it edits messily. With its inability to completely remove marks, it leaves behind a faint tracery of the evolution of an idea, of the steps and missteps leading to the final solution. I often find ideas and even beauty in the mess.

It is essential for an organization that values creative thinking to ensure that as much work as possible remains visible and available to everyone. At GM, concepts that didn't look promising were edited out early. Assistant studio chiefs felt it their responsibility to remove any sign of misdirected effort lest it offend the eyes of the chief, who then further edited the material, and so on up the chain of command. At any point during a project, the progress was to appear smooth and steady. The widely held assumption was that an error-free process would more reliably lead to error-free results. As it turns out, this was not an error-free position.

At NDI, the questionable attempts and even the out-and-out boners are often displayed side-by-side with the obviously promising directions for the duration of a project. It is not that the managers lack discrimination or are reluctant to tell it as it is to the staff, but rather that they function more like kneaded erasers than dispensers of opaque correction fluid as they work their way through the process.

* * *

Avoiding failure whenever possible is an eminently reasonable goal for business. However, a preoccupation with its avoidance *while casting around for novel ideas* presents a serious impediment to the creative process. Considerable effort must be made to breed a culture not only tolerant of blunders and miscalculations, but one demonstrating an appreciation of their worth. Excessive fear of failure does not yield the kind of confidence required for the act of creation, perhaps the ultimate act of human optimism.

"This is going *nowhere!*" barks Alfonso Albaisa unexpectedly to the gods from deep within the helter-skelter jungle of his preferred working environs. This is usually followed by a trenchantly vile-sounding string of explicatives in his native Cuban-inflected Spanish, surely *the* universal swearing language of choice. A highly intuitive designer, he cries out in some similar fashion at virtually the same point in every project. In response to these eruptions, someone either reinforces the promise of his original glimmer in the hope he will not abandon it, or picks up the idea himself.

While Albaisa's cry might at times be nothing more than the kind of late-night release commonly heard and ignored in college dorms, in an hospitable environment it can also serve as an invitation. Infusing and sustaining a cultural climate receptive to engaging with and openly using each other's work and struggles, mistakes and all, demands considerable effort from NDI's management. New employees are inevitably skeptical that we actually work in this way and need reassurance over time to overcome their deeply embedded suspicion. We therefore have an ever-expanding menu of strategies to provoke creative interplay.

Sometimes a group is assembled from various studios to simultaneously attack the same problem. When we needed a crop of novel and varied ideas to kick-start the Altima project in Blue Studio, designers from throughout the building were gathered together for a week. Their desks were arranged in a tight circle. It was bedlam, but great fun, like an idea picnic with everyone nibbling from one another's desks. This "circling the wagons," which we have come to call it, did *not* yield a batch of similar ideas, as might have been expected. Rather, it was as though each person was motivated to try something *unlike* what they saw developing around them. Exposure to their colleagues' work stimulated the making of sharp distinctions at least as much as it did the forging of connections with it.

Other times, when individuals are laboring independently and seem mired down on the paths they've taken, the managers will suggest swapping them midstream, taking on the assumptions and challenges of each other's directions. Management is often surprised at how relieved people are to throw themselves into a different set of issues for a while. They may occasionally return to their original tasks refreshed by a different orientation and some badly needed distance, or find themselves committed to the new path.

At still other times, someone will offer up ideas that have stymied them but seem worth further exploration. Bruce Campbell had come up with an intriguing way of packaging six passengers for a commuter car prioritizing comfort; three rows of two seats rather than the conventional two rows of three. However, this made for a proportionally long, narrow vehicle, and in shaping a form around this arrangement, he found himself confronting something that looked a great deal like a banana on wheels.

Casting his head to one side and gingerly holding out the sketch with the tips of his fingers as though it was impregnated with some foul-smelling substance, he walked into the Red Studio one morning and let it drop onto Tom Semple's desk. "Maybe *you* can do something with this!" he said, turning and walking away, knowing Semple loved the challenge of transforming nearly anything into something beautiful. Recognizing his own limits at that moment, Campbell's open acknowledgment of his "failure" led to a fruitful utilization of the combined talents of the staff. That banana-on-wheels became the Cocoon, an important concept vehicle for us, and as with the Pulsar NX, it was hard to know whom to credit with its design.

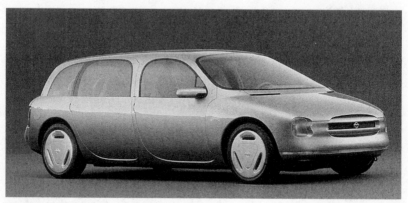

"Cocoon" prototype

We know things are going well when we have a hard time tracing the ancestry of our ideas. However, we spend considerable time recounting their histories, being sure to acknowledge the developers, key critics, supporters, and finishers as well as the instigators. This is vital in allaying any fears about receiving proper credit in the kind of diffuse environment being proposed. Surprisingly, there is less concern than might have been expected. Ideas are like a virus: They spread far and fast, and it is easy to spot the host and the carriers. Unlike having a virus, however, having an idea is immensely pleasurable and self-rewarding. Still, there must be genuine appreciation and recognition of the diverse skills and tasks required for realizing prototypical thinking.

As with the various instrumentalists in my little rock band, each contribution, from failed attempts to brilliant insights, serves a vital yet distinct role in creating the rhythm, harmony, and texture of the final product. Acknowledgment and commendation help to break down the presumed one-to-one correspondence between career success and solitary achievement. While ideas are conceived in individual minds, they are seldom born in isolation and rarely realized alone.

* * *

Failures and errors made by individuals within the group present one set of issues for the *creative priority* that can be dealt with through individual interactions. Failure by the group as a whole, or even the company itself, makes for a different order of challenge, and presents further opportunities for breakthrough thinking.

Fueled by the sheer exhilaration of its formative years and a strong desire to prove its worth to the parent company, NDI was inspired to introduce a new and impactful line of cars into an increasingly crowded and competitive field in the early and mid-eighties. The Hardbody trucks—Pathfinder, Pulsar NX, and others—generated considerable sales and helped establish southern California as a new center of international automobile design. They also secured a place for the new satellite within Nissan's global network.

Tired of a certain Detroit design aroma then prevailing, what we had termed an aesthetics of excess, the original staff was further motivated to develop a rare (for American cars) aesthetics of efficiency, of doing the most with the least. This direction was consonant with what we most admired about the Japanese manufacturers and their extraordinary accomplishments in engineering and production efficiencies. We created designs with a quality of exposed structuralism—something we referred to as an "exo-structure"—that, combined with taut but subtly nuanced three-dimensional forms, established what was referred to in the press as an "NDI look." We had achieved a signature style.

With the successes of our early efforts, the company was dramatically expanded to more than twice its original size as it took on a whole new spate of projects in the late eighties. A fresh generation of talent introduced new attitudes, expectations, and personal missions. And as work began on our second generation of projects, it was with considerably more confidence and a secure sense of ourselves. We immediately began to refine and further evolve the direction we had established.

But when the early concepts for these products were presented in Japan, for the first time we sensed some reserve and disappointment. NDI had already exposed the parent company to a whole new world of design possibilities, and Nissan was eager for more. Not, however, more of the same. There was no element of discovery or surprise in the new offerings, which to our eyes represented another level of maturity and refinement. We were sure it was a cultural thing.

Even more disquieting was the reaction of all the new members of the staff. They agreed with the Japanese, and had been trying to tell us all along through their designs, which had been misread by management as failed attempts to "get with the program." What we heard stung and stopped us in our tracks. Somehow, at some point, the "NDI look" had become the "NDI smell," and we'd not detected it ourselves. This was no cultural thing.

We learned that the original core group of designers had even acquired a name with the new generation: "Mount Rushmore." We were now the establishment, our style seen as being carved in stone and impervious to change. It was unsettling that, in so short a time, our ideas had come to represent the old guard. But the early battles had been fought and won. They did not represent the issues of this new generation, who came happily into an existing, established sandbox to realize their own visions and fight their own battles.

We took a good look around us, stepped back from the canvas we had been creating for others, and began to realize we were failing, or afraid, to use it ourselves. We had become trapped in the all-too-familiar business of fighting old enemies long after they had ceased to be of any concern to anyone else. The designs we had created somehow came to symbolize the very freedom of our experience at NDI, and we mistakenly had begun to overprotect them.

Most of all, we had stopped playing with the ideas, risking abandoning them altogether to tackle new and unknown obstacles. We should have noted the lack of play. But we didn't, and as a result the managers agreed to enter, or reenter, a state of healthy uncertainty, soul-searching, and path-finding, with the new staff helping to lead the way.

Leaving behind an established and successful design paradigm left us feeling naked and at risk. But new directions began to emerge, at first slowly. Cars such as the Quest, Altima, and Infiniti J30 were born, cars that had nothing to do with the exo-structure or form-vocabulary of our previous products. And there is yet another cluster of products currently being developed in the studios that will be seen on the road around the turn of the century. What also emerged from this experience was a heightened alertness to those pivotal moments, usually hidden by success, when an otherwise healthy body of thought begins to ossify into doctrine. When a style becomes a smell.

Confronting our errors openly, overcoming our defensiveness and embarrassment, and modeling the same behavior we were expecting from the staff all helped to reinforce an atmosphere tolerant of failure. It also enabled us to open doors that would have remained closed, at least until the greater and more costly failures that might have occurred had we continued on our original path. This can only happen in a culture more concerned with the potential lurking in failure than in the mere avoidance of its repercussions.

Toppling someone else's blocks to clear the way for building a new tower turns out to be far less difficult than toppling your own.

***

In all these strategies to stimulate idea-sharing and interplay, there is a common theme: play itself. In searching for ideas, we play around with them, turning them upside down, inside-out, mirror-imaged, and backwards, toying with the possibilities the way children do instinctively. Watching a child search (not re-search) for an understanding of the way something works with characteristic optimism, unselfconscious abandon, and equal measures of frustration and joy is a fine means of recapturing the spirit vital to original thinking. Creating can be elusive, frustrating, and plain hard work. But it also has a necessary quality of abandon and re-creation about it.

Work tends to be a convergent activity, focusing in on the task at hand. Play is a divergent activity. It opens out and is not easy to contain. At NDI, we have deliberately made room for it, and it is often difficult to know when we are using play to work or when we are simply playing while at work. So we don't worry much about it.

Some remarkable (and remarkably silly) pranks, practical jokes, and other apparently nonsensical events are continually played out at NDI. One day a set of antique bowling pins appeared at one end of our long, narrow courtyard. No one to this day claims to know who bought them or placed them there, or why. The next day, they were found lined up, spaced evenly along the roughly three-hundred-foot length of the courtyard. The following week they disappeared, only to be spotted along the top ledges of the buildings that run the length of the courtyard on either side. The pins continued to mysteriously move around the building, each new setting more intriguing than the last. This lasted months, culminating in their touching arrangement around the sides of a little reflecting pool with a small waterfall. Here, a clearly drowned pin floated alone, solemnly observed by all the other pins lined up attentively along the edge, each wedged so that it tilted forward ever so slightly, looking remarkably remorseful. No one ever claimed credit for any of these staged, site-specific bowling pin events, but everyone knew that everyone else was involved. And the subject was never discussed. The pins finally vanished for at least a year, only to appear again for yet another series of curious, clever, funny, and really stupid arrangements.

If I do not mention the most infamous prank of all, I will be thought cowardly, as I was its target. I was called to the shop one day just before lunch to see a prototype, and therefore did not see anything ominous in the fact that no one was around. Tom Semple and others were with me as we looked at the model, when suddenly all the corrugated metal doors that spanned almost one hundred feet of the shop wall began to rock violently in unison. Simultaneously, a network of ceiling-mounted heating and air-conditioning hoses decoupled and spewed hissing steam all over the place. A split second later, a rack of twenty-foot steel tubing began clattering noisily to the cement floor. It was clearly a major earthquake. I instinctively ducked, yelling out something about this being "the big one, the worst one I'd ever experienced," and raced outside. Meanwhile, Tom Semple reacted in his typically stoic fashion. He slowly looked around, John Wayne–like, and calmly ambled out.

All this time, someone was lying out of sight in the shop, recording the goings-on with a video camera in hand. It was all a massive hoax involving a synchronized cast of corrugated-door rockers, vent-hose liberators, rack-tippers, and other conspirators all programmed at their various staging centers with split-second timing, watches preset like those of a precision SWAT team.

Before knowing this, I staunchly denied ever having said it was the worst quake I'd ever "felt." I had said "experienced," which I saw as being somehow less embarrassing. Furthermore, I claimed to have moved instinctively to herd my colleagues out of harm's way. But they had the tape, you see. And it shows me looking more like a cross between John Belushi and Charlie Chaplin responding to some off-screen, oncoming disaster. It is kept hidden somewhere and shown only at the most awkward possible moments.

There are countless other such meaningless pranks and carryings on whose description could easily fill another book. But the point is that risking and seriously playing around with ideas is easy in such an atmosphere. Furthermore, playing around with ideas in turn engenders such an atmosphere. Neither creativity nor play will remain in their separate ponds for long. Their ripples, if they are allowed, will spread out, effecting what Silvano Arieti has called a "creativogenic" (in the sense of photogenic or telegenic) situation.[2] All of which leads Linda to ask, "Do you folks ever actually do any *real work* around there?"

We do. Really, we do. But creative play is such a quixotic, fleeting, and, well, playful business that it is difficult to come up with concrete examples of how this spirit yields important results. But it does, continually.

At an early mindmap session for the Infiniti J30 luxury car, we were trying to enunciate the kind of identity we wanted the car to have, as well as imagine the people we wanted it to attract. Many of our best sessions (they're not all good) tend to begin with humor. We are not always sure why, but we go with the impulse and jot or sketch everything onto a large sheet of paper. This particular pow-wow began with an off-color story I no longer recall, but I do remember the toilet bowl someone sketched to remind us of its punch line. Only later did we realize that it was the abstract form of the bowl itself, its voluminous, fully rounded, stable, and organic shape that brought the joke to mind in the first place. The associated imagery helped us to identify the nonverbal form-vocabulary we felt was right for this product.

Later in the same session, we began conjuring just who it was that would be willing to spend the kind of money this car would cost. More than just gathering quantified data and dry demographics about them, we wanted to understand and bring to life the character and demeanor of people who might be attracted to such a product, in much the manner of method actors, and then design it for ourselves in that role. (It is important to know here that we were designing this car in the mid-eighties, when yuppiedom reigned supreme.) Whether designing for truckers, surfers, or investment bankers, reaching for this kind of understanding of the intended users of our products brings a level of empathy that seems to pinpoint the nuances and keep the product "in character."

As colorful anecdotes, adjectives, and sketches began filling the board, a comically hyperbolic caricature of our J30 buyer began to emerge. We imagined the kind of self-assured, entirely too fit person who would pull up next to us at a light in a mirror-polished, irritatingly clean car wearing an outfit color-coordinated with it, an equally flawless member of the opposite sex next to them, each probably closing deals on matching cell phones, and an exotic dog sheared like some elaborate topiary in the back seat—the kind of person we would not want to give the pleasure of seeing us gawking.

For shorthand, we labeled this quintessential J30 buyer "the perfect asshole!" Of course, all of this was playfully irreverent and exaggerated (*wildly* exaggerated, for all the J30 owners reading this). But it was precisely this mock impudence and flouting of the more generic descriptions ("upwardly mobile," "nouveau riche," "class-conscious," and the like) that enabled us to break through the stereotypes and freely access the associations and imagery we needed for inspiration.

Having broken through, we were then able to further tune and nail down the hoped-for expression of the car. We saw that it should be androgynous (appealing to both of those cell-phone users), understated, and detailed to perfection, both inside and out. The surfaces should be modulated so that the highlights and reflections would leap to life with the level of polishing they would surely enjoy. We wanted every gesture to seem necessary, as though changing any element would destroy the whole. While we realized it was not in the Japanese scheme of things to have this car last for decades unchanged, we aimed for the timelessness of a classic. And we aimed for the fluid, sensual, elegantly sculptured forms reminiscent of those on the underappreciated underside of the lowly toilet bowl we had earlier jokingly flashed on.

✳ ✳ ✳

The business of imagining a new idea into existence requires a fusion of discipline and abandon, of stubborn determination and childlike openness to serendipity, of a drive to succeed and a comfort with failure. There is always a leap of faith, even a naïveté, in going with a notion that has no precedent or prior reality.

Most of the time while we search for a car among the lines lying loosely all over the vellum page, the images remain inert. Still. Car-shaped pillows and car-shaped bricks. Static and soundless and flat. Then, every once in a while, the vellum comes alive, the white page now white space, the lines now edges to palpable forms that lock into focus and take shape. A real vehicle begins to emerge just under the pens, pastels, and markers, all of which now move with a certainty and urgency of their own. At these moments, the designer is a smiling, almost passive observer, a child again playing with cars, a willing passenger on a ride seemingly fueled by someone else. And it is then that sounds are likely to emerge from the designer's throat—low, raunchy growls, the sounds of engines purring, revving, and howling. Working has turned into making-believe has turned into making.

PART III

Beyond the Edges

I begin to wonder how many things I know that would suddenly take on new meaning if only I could perceive the connections. I foresee a restless night.

Robert Scott Root-Bernstein[1]

7

The Blurring of Disciplinary Boundaries

"We're gonna need a bigger boat!" bellowed someone over the growing din in Red Studio as it launched into the design of the first-generation Quest minivan. The infamous phrase from the movie *Jaws* aptly described the overcrowded conditions as engineers, modelers, interior and exterior designers, shop personnel, and researchers crawled over one another to do their work. But the thinly disguised fear of sinking suggested by Roy Scheider's memorable line did not accurately capture the wonderful buoyancy of all the agitation and energy afloat in the studio. We have long looked back on this project as a joyous model of creative ferment.

The Quest assignment was as complex as any NDI had yet encountered. It represented Nissan's first entry into a segment of the rapidly growing utility market, and the design would have to further satisfy the needs of the Ford Motor Company which, in a complex arrangement with Nissan, would market the car as the Mercury Villager with only minor adjustments. So we had two clients from two distinct galaxies, the second-largest automakers in their respective countries, and neither shy about expressing their positions. Perhaps a battleship . . .

Both companies had agreed to form a temporary partnership to defray the staggering costs of introducing a new line of vehicles that each needed. In a complicated contract, Nissan was to be responsible for the design, which would be done in San Diego, and the engineering, which would be done at its Research and Development facility (NRD) in Farmington Hills, Michigan. Ford would be responsible for the manufacturing at its plant in Avon Lake, Ohio. Final decisions would be made conjointly in Dearborn, San Diego, and Tokyo. Perhaps an aircraft carrier . . .

Determined to avoid as much of the inevitable political haggling as possible, we threw ourselves into the business of framing the project, defining the vehicle in our own terms (which is mandatory even when there are acceptable existing definitions), embodying a "minivan mind-set," and commencing to search for its soul.

Chrysler's boxy and bland minivan then dominated the market virtually without competition, having seized the initiative in the early eighties. Neither GM nor Toyota had yet entered the fray, and Ford was represented by its ineptly designed Aerostar. The NDI designers were eager to rid the van of its characterless, commercial image. They saw no reason why something primarily useful in nature needed to be boring or uninteresting.

Interior and exterior design activities traditionally occupy different workspaces. But with the minivan, a vehicle whose interior design was deemed critical to its success, NDI wanted to make certain that this aspect received all the attention it deserved. Customers have often (and properly) complained when the character and quality of the inside and outside of a vehicle do not match. It is always disconcerting to climb into a sleek sports car only to feel like you have inadvertently entered some adolescent video-game parlor, or ease into a high-performance touring sedan to encounter all the romance of an endodontist's waiting room. Yet, since the design was inevitably done by different people in different workspaces, this was really not so surprising. What *was* surprising was that no one had thought to address the integration of the product by integrating the process. So, at the risk of overloading the system, we simply merged the interior and exterior design efforts on this project into one bustling studio. The limits of what had previously been considered the inside or outside of the vehicle were deliberately obscured.

As the staff began familiarizing themselves with the fixed hardware (powerplant, suspension type, body construction, etc.), the character of the market, and the aims of the vehicle's two manufacturers, some of the designers began sketching what the industry called a "one-box" shape. Rather than the traditional "two-box" configuration, this one featured a dramatic windshield that sloped smoothly into the hood in a single, continuous arc. The sketches illustrated minivans with an exotic rocket-ship-on-wheels appearance that certainly didn't look like commercial delivery vans. As the concepts were stapled up onto the display board, they attracted immediate attention, not all of it positive.

Without a formal meeting having been called, a spontaneous discussion erupted around the sketches, as numerous and sundry frames of reference focused in on the same issues. "Does this configuration do anything for us?" challenged an interior designer of the exterior designers. "Since we've defined a minivan as a large, flexible interior volume on four wheels," continued an engineer, "shouldn't we be designing this thing from the inside out?" "What the hell would it feel like driving it?" asked another. If anyone from the parent company had walked in during this back-and-forth, they would have understandably wondered just who was running the show.

Before the gathering had dispersed, there was agreement to build a quick, crude, but accurate full-size mock-up of a one-box van we could climb into in order to evaluate the concept while sitting inside. Within a day, an ad hoc team comprising people from each of the disciplines concocted what looked like a model airplane frame before the paper skin was stretched over it. This "seating buck" consisted of a large slab of plywood the size of the minivan's floor plan, a block of Styrofoam located where the engine would be, and three rows of seats bolted in place. A series of foamcore cross-sectional templates was then arrayed along the length of the beast like a webbing of skeletal ribs, all held in place by a central spine delineating its side-view profile. The entire cardboard/plywood/foamcore affair, fastened together by duct tape, glue, and staples, was then jerryrigged onto four truck tires we had lying around.

The studio was a mess, but out of the bedlam had emerged what looked like the reconstructed skeletal remains of some ancient creature bound for a museum of vehicular anthropology. It was crude, but managed to convey both the exterior and interior volumes accurately.

The following morning the mock-up was rolled outside into the viewing courtyard. By this time, most of NDI had become curious about all the turmoil in Red Studio and joined the review of the concept. Viewed from afar, it suggested something potentially exciting and exotic. But then, as everyone climbed inside, its appeal rapidly evaporated. As a result of the extreme angle and forward position of the pillars framing the windshield, visibility was badly blocked. The useless expanse of interior volume between the fast-sloping windshield and the absurdly deep dashpanel would be difficult to heat and cool and nearly impossible to clean. Certainly, nothing could be stored in the extra space provided. And sitting in the driver's position felt like driving a bus from the middle row of seats. The entire direction was unanimously rejected out of hand.

When GM later introduced its racy Pontiac and Oldsmobile minivans featuring their one-box shapes, they met with instant and harsh rejection. Inspired by an earlier showcar called the Transport, the company proudly proclaimed that its vans had been designed "from the outside in." For a product whose principal purpose was the provision of practical and useful interior space, their designs boldly celebrated a new vehicle sporting impractical and useless volume— hardly the right message to send to buyers of such vehicles.

Due to the early involvement of all participants speaking freely across disciplinary bounds at NDI, a potentially disastrous error was easily avoided. Further development time spent on a one-box mini-van would have generated commitment, resistance to change, and a misguided waste of energy. Instead, the studio had welded into a variegated team, the edges of whose individual activities and responsibilities had been intentionally blurred. The overlapping dynamics of the process had prompted the early identification of a fundamental weakness in the concept, and further sharpened the group's notions of what a minivan should (and shouldn't) be.

When a small group of designers was returning from lunch one afternoon, they spotted a disgruntled couple wrestling the cumbersome, heavy seats out of their minivan. It was clear that the large interior volume promised by the exterior design was neither flexible nor accessible, and the problem lodged itself in the designers' minds. Within days, an idea was born. The idea of designing seats that folded easily into a vertical format and then slid on extended tracks came into being. There were already tracks under the front seats of cars allowing for about six inches of adjustment for legroom. Why, we wondered, couldn't the six inches become six feet, so that the owners could easily transform the passenger space into a capacious hauling space without having to unbolt and remove the seats? The Quest could then truly provide both flexible and accessible interior volume.

Everyone from every department joined in to install a working prototype of this folding/sliding seat arrangement. Out of this turmoil the Quest Trac system was born, an industry first. The involvement across departmental bounds further clarified what our minivan should be in everyone's mind, and the interior began leading the exterior design, a highly appropriate process for such a vehicle.

Shop personnel and technicians, traditionally underutilized sources of innovation, became deeply involved in resolving critical aspects of the concept as well as the mechanism. People who make also think; and once made aware that their ideas matter, they can bring a uniquely hands-on kind of inventiveness to a project. John Toom, the manager of NDI's extensive metal, plastic, and wood shops, and his highly seasoned crew share the credit on many of NDI's patents, and were full creative partners in bringing the flexible seating system to fruition.

The engineers had become involved in conceiving the vehicle's shape. The designers had engaged themselves in the complex business of package engineering. Exterior designers were helping to shape the interior, and the interior designers were affecting the exterior forms. The modelers were not only building the model, they were also inventing a quick and ingenious tool for measuring the three-dimensional architecture of a vehicle, something we have continued to use at the beginning of every project since that time. Everyone in the project had become involved in everyone else's business, and Nissan proudly proclaimed in its advertising that its new minivans had been designed from the inside out.

***

When interviewing prospective candidates, we generally like to discover their attitudes towards fences. Do they favor distinct borderlines? Is it important to them that others mind their own business, and do they prefer minding their own? If the answers are strongly in the affirmative, a little caution light goes on.

We go on to ask how they would feel working at a place where meddling across departmental borders is encouraged, where people outside their own areas of expertise would be freely commenting on their work, and where they in turn would be expected to become involved in the efforts of other disciplines they may know little about.

Most organizations work hard to establish and maintain clear lines of responsibility between positions, occupations, and departments. Formal definitions are kept on file, and evaluations and raises are based principally on performance within these bounds. This clarity and discreteness are further reinforced by architectural and geographic separation. At the Nissan Technical Center in Atsugi, Japan, engineers, designers, and modelers all occupy their own offices, studios, and buildings, which reflect the diverse nature of their work. Everything about the arrangement is crisp, clean, and logical. Appointments are made when meetings are required and there is little chance of disorder. Curiously, next to the engineering/ design building is a substantial edifice called the Simultaneous Engineering Building. Simultaneity, it seems, must also be scheduled.

The *efficiency priority* demands a file-drawer approach to organizational design, everyone clearly accountable for work within their own domains, with as little overlap or redundancy as possible. The goal is to make everything function with the clockwork precision suggested by the "org chart," separate boxes of activity connected by straight lines, all very black and white, sequential yet discontinuous and unrelated.

When considering its own chart, NDI perceives the white space on the page between, outside, and around all the little boxes and lines as neither so flat, inert, or empty as it appears. The diagram is seen as a dynamic, multidimensional, overlapping, and continually adjusting flux of activities and responsibilities. There are, of course, job definitions, but these include relational considerations and expected areas of interaction and shared responsibilities.

The *creative priority* requires a grayer, more ambiguous and layered arrangement that offers the possibility of disorder, reorder, and new order. For this reason, most of the disciplines at the company are gathered into the same large spaces. Even those whose needs demand their own environments (administration, the shops, the paint department, for example) are encouraged to spend considerable time in the studios. From the outset, these studio spaces were developed as hubs, centers of intersecting priorities and activities without barriers or fences. Narrow lines of communication were replaced by broad, teeming zones of cohabitation.

Each discipline, of course, continues to have its own agenda, workstyle, and rhythm. But its borders are kept deliberately vague. This is not always so comfortable. While turf wars over departmentally entrenched positions are significantly reduced, as was the case with the interior versus exterior requirements of the Quest, there is a potential increase in interpersonal friction. Many feel insecure and threatened working within the fuzzy logic of such a system. Not only is it necessary to engage in the usual business of carving out one's own space in the company, there are the additional stresses of carving into someone else's, who will in turn be expected to be slicing into your own. In this sense, however, *blurring the boundaries* expands the prospects for surprising conjunctions, unforeseen opportunities, and *creative abrasion*.

❊ ❊ ❊

When negotiating over the forms at the leading edge of a hood during a trip to Japan with one of Nissan's aerodynamic engineers, I expressed discomfort with what his drawings suggested. The surface development was out of character with the design direction that had been established. We both knew that aerodynamics was as much a "black art" as a hard science, and that there were many ways to manipulate form in order to achieve efficient airflow.

Nonetheless, he felt crowded by this intrusion into his world, and he let me know. After all, he had the responsibility of attaining a specific numerical target of aerodynamic efficiency called the "coefficient of drag." At the same time, as the car's designer, NDI had the responsibility of achieving a more difficult to quantify but equally important coefficient of beauty.

We agreed to continue working together on the issue, and the following day the engineer arranged for me to see the forms I was insisting on in Nissan's state-of-the-art wind tunnel. By injecting an inky vapor into the roughly two-hundred-mph airflow, it was easy to see its path over the hoodforms, and it was not a pretty sight. Rather than smoothly attaching itself to the surface, the air separated and erupted into a chaotic, ugly, and obviously inefficient turbulence, a turbulence that would increase drag and windnoise while decreasing fuel efficiency. Our forms no longer looked so attractive to me.

By continuing to work back and forth between the design studio and the wind tunnel, however, we eventually achieved a solution both attractive and efficient. The traditional war between automobile designers and engineers over whether aerodynamics is an engineering responsibility (it is) or a design responsibility (it is) yielded to a more fruitful, realistic, and streamlined overlapping of activities. When given our design briefs for a project, designers as well as engineers are now informed of the numerical targets for aerodynamic efficiency. It is a shared, if somewhat blurred, commission. But by formally extending the responsibilities of certain tasks beyond the confines of a single department, Nissan increases the likelihood that a product's components will function simultaneously on a broader number of planes.

The car certainly doesn't care who is responsible for which part. And neither does the customer.

* * *

As I was moved into management rather early in my career at GM, I didn't feel ready to stop doing what I loved: designing. Flattered that they saw enough in my ideas to move me into a position of responsibility, I was also surprised that the corporation would even *want* me to stop generating them. I recall sneaking in drawing time as a chief, continuing to interact creatively with the studio in between visits of "the suits." Of course, once promoted, I never again signed a sketch at GM.

While it is ordinarily difficult to trace the origins of a colloquialism, I feel pretty certain that the use of the term "suits," as in "the suits are coming," began in the long hallways between the studios at GM Styling in the early sixties. Those executives in three-piece suits roaming the halls to monitor the work and fill the seats around meeting tables were once, we knew, all designers, people who entered the field with some passion and skills and had chalk dust and ink stains somewhere on them.

Once promoted, however, it was necessary to dress and act like an executive, and that meant abandoning the chalk and the pens. And so, at the presumed peak of their creative potential, legions of talent ceased doing what they did best.

When I challenged this prescription during my first evaluation as a studio chief, I was told it was now time to leave behind that stage of my career. What I heard them saying was, it was now time to leave behind childish things. "A staff should be staffing, a manager managing," I was reprimanded, and I really "shouldn't have time for anything else."

Upon leaving Detroit, those I brought with me to form the nucleus of NDI all shared a deep passion for their work, and we were all committed to finding a way to remain active designers, modelers, or engineers while still managing to manage. Since creativity was our agreed-upon priority, that was really the only option, and we committed ourselves to meet any problems this engendered head-on.

Our playing-managers began turning out some of the finest work of their careers. But over time, as new, younger staff were added, we began to see some problems. While they respected and were inspired by their more experienced bosses, and even sensed that their own work would be fairly selected if a choice had to be made, a subtle and insidious laxity had begun to creep in. The designs tended to have a passive look, like they were done knowing the chiefs would step in to refine, correct, and resolve them. They just did not look ready for prime time. With so much creative horse-power engaged above them, there was not the sense of ownership or urgency that results in the stringent self-monitoring so necessary for concept-making.

The managers at first regarded all these inadequately focused concepts as simply the best efforts of inexperienced designers. Later, they thought it was perhaps "a generational thing." As it turned out, it was neither.

We tried stepping back from the process, using staff ideas when-ever possible, and our skills mostly to assist and nurture. This helped, but there still wasn't the sense of focus and serious intent about the ideas we wanted to see. Over time, the workload increased and the creative output of the staff became increasingly important. Stopping the managers from doing active design work was now out of the question, and we felt stymied.

One day, Tom Semple walked into my office with an oblique approach to the problem, one simultaneously appealing and threat-ening—always a hopeful combination. "I was thinking about the designers self-assigning their projects," he suggested. While it sounded simple enough, this idea represented a significant depar-ture from traditional automotive design management, one we had already departed from significantly. At GM, not only were projects assigned by management, even the *types* of vehicles any one designer could work on were predetermined. Within the first few years, an individual was often identified as either an exterior or interior designer, then slotted as being more suited to working on cars, trucks, vans, sedans, luxury cars, or sports cars—for life. "He's a van guy" or "a natural trucker" or "a pure sports car animal" were common phrases used to pigeonhole and stereotype someone as a specialist in a given area.

At NDI, while we used everyone for virtually everything, it had still been the responsibility of management to assign projects to the studios. Which studio got which project was usually a matter of mere scheduling. It was just a question of who was finished with the previous assignment and ready to go. The staff were reassigned every three or four years in order to work with different people in a different environment, sometimes switched between interior and exterior responsibilities. It was all done thoughtfully, but it was all done *for* them. What Semple was now proffering was that it be done *by* them, or at the very least, *with* them.

Presented with the available menu of work at a given point in time, each would select a project according to what piqued their interest. The hope was that the increased sense of control of their daily worklives, as well as the heightened motivation from involvement with what intrinsically attracted them, would offset the sense of distance from the end results of their work that we had detected.

By and large, it worked. With only minor adjustments necessary to make sure there was adequate balance, each project was attacked with great zeal. The appeal of self-selection was so high that even "buddies" did not stick together. Instead, combinations of personalities gathered together to form teams we would never have thought to make. The glue was the work itself. And that was the key.

As with all good ideas, this one brought with it a host of good new problems, "good problems" being defined as ones accompanying an otherwise worthwhile new concept that elevated it to a higher plane. In this case, we had moved from dealing with the problems of oppression to those associated with greater freedom.

For Chris Lee, a feisty Korean-American designer who had been struggling hard to find his own "voice," this shift in methodology proved pivotal. He had been somewhat tentative during his early years with NDI, always waiting for management input and approval. "I started thinking more about what pleased *me* rather than the executives," he said, "and since it was *my* project, it just kind of happened." Lee's work took a big leap. Ironically, as he began taking his own voice more seriously and had less need of management approval, management at the same time began to take his work more seriously.

To Alfonso Albaisa, for whom autonomy is central, this new procedure was enormously liberating. "I'll work here now until death or retirement, whichever comes first!" he exclaimed. For others, there were some reservations. A few felt they might tend to lean towards projects due to their familiarity, thereby missing out on exposure to something unexpectedly appealing. Others liked the established camaraderie of existing teams. Even some members of management were not at first thrilled. Diane Allen had worked hard to establish her "Red Studio family," which was indeed a high-functioning group. This new procedure would occasionally break apart established teams within studio bounds. But even she has grown to appreciate the fresh perspectives and unexpected personnel couplings it offers.

Overall, however, Semple's concept has been adopted and well received. It is not used all the time, but the fact of its availability seems to be a source of great energy and motivation for the staff.

What is significant here is that this process was born out of a willingness to *blur the boundaries* separating staff from management. The examples of the principle thus far presented in this chapter have all been on a horizontal plane, those between disciplines and departments. Its creative potential, however, works as well on a vertical plane, between the upper reaches of staff autonomy and the lower reaches of managerial authority.

By having the supervisors and chiefs continue to design, we had already blurred this boundary, but in only one direction: downward. This self-selection procedure provided a necessary counterbalance: blurring the line from the bottom up as well.

It might seem uncomfortable at first to some managers, who might feel they are relinquishing a portion of their power. But it remains necessary for management to modulate and remain intimately involved in the process. Each project presents its own agenda, and we find ourselves continuing to evolve and refine the way it works.

As with all applications of this priority, it is fuzzy. Deliberately so. Each layer in an organization will jealously guard the extent of its authority and power. But it will just as rigorously monitor its limits in order to avoid responsibility for anything beyond its prescribed domain.

There are what seem to be two mutually contradictory and often-heard cries from within an organization. On the one hand, there is a reasonable plea for clear understanding of the responsibilities and limits of a job, position, or department. On the other hand, there is an urgent need to feel connected with the overall picture and the end product. These are not necessarily conflicting positions. But in our zeal for clarity, and our need to avoid failure outside the realm of our presumed areas of accountability, we tend to overdefine our roles and thus build barriers and fences precisely where there need to be bridges, windows, and doors.

Just as the imagination knows no bounds, so an organization prizing innovation must penetrate and soften the perimeters. These edges constitute the very connective tissue that holds an organization together. And it is precisely within this vague region between well-defined zones that most creative ideas occur.

The only thing that suffers is the comforting clarity of the organization chart.

***

We had a family "great man." He was Morris Dann, the eldest of my mother's siblings and the only one born in "the old country." A self-educated man who had never had the opportunity to attend college or even graduate high school, he went on to become a noted inventor, engineer, and precursor of an entirely new profession.

With a natural mechanical bent and insatiable curiosity, he was hired as a lab technician by the Department of Pharmacology at the Medical School of Western Reserve University in Cleveland in the early 1920s. He quickly began to grasp the rudiments of medicine, and absorbed the nature of the groundbreaking research going on around him at the time, devising equipment to demonstrate the principles of pharmacology, as well as tools for its research. This required him to develop expertise in everything from welding and electronics to photographic development, and even glassblowing for test tubes and custom vials for the labs.

Uncle Morris was an incorrigible gatherer of widgets, thingumajigs, and gizmos. During his spare time, he used to love prowling around five-and-dimes and hardware stores, picking up intriguing hinges, handles, levers, locks, toys, clocks, corks, tubing, rubber hose, pieces of glass, and other doohickeys. While he had no conscious need for them at the time of purchase, he would stash them in cabinets filled with little wooden compartments and drawers in his growing shop at the university.

Over time, he became an increasingly vital part of the ongoing research and educational programs. And he began tinkering with the traditional and often badly outmoded tools of medicine and research, as well as concocting ones that had never been imagined. For a kymograph, a biological monitoring device, he ingeniously used an alarm clock mechanism to power the drums of paper on which various reactions (pulse rate, blood pressure, etc.) would be recorded. He smoked the paper with kerosene lamps which would then allow pinpoint scratches from the recording needle to register as clean white lines. When measuring pressure, he needed a reliable diaphragm, and for this he used the most trustworthy membrane available in his cabinets: a condom. It was a state-of-the-art device at the time.

He went on to generate dozens of innovations, including making key contributions to the development of the first disposable hypodermic syringe, for which he holds several patents. Most significantly for me, he created the infant resuscitator, a pathbreaking instrument for aiding newborns in taking their first breath. We are all born with "collapsed" lungs, and not all of us can generate enough energy to distend them the first time. The resuscitator was a major advance over a slap on the behind. The device was powered with great effectiveness by a Trico windshield-wiper motor from one of his drawers. His son, Norman, later manufactured and distributed it as the Dann Resuscitator.

An engineer/entrepreneur with a business acumen his father never possessed, Norman Dann went on to build one of the vanguard companies in the budding field of medical instrumentation. And he gave me my first professional design commission in 1962 for the design of the resuscitator while I was still in design school, an assignment that piqued a fascination with medical instruments that continues for me to this day.

Mechanics and hard engineering were fields at the time more closely associated with cars, heavy machinery, and bridges. With his technological skills and an ever-growing grasp of the elements of medicine and pharmacology, Morris Dann became a pioneer in what would later emerge as the hybrid field of medical engineering, two words never before connected. Previous connections, however, were not his principal concern. New ones were.

Of course, he would never have felt comfortable being called a pioneer. When approached to join the Society of Biological Engineers near the end of his career, he turned them down, feeling inadequately educated to belong. "Hell, I'm just the first guy to put a machine shop in a medical school," he insisted.

He had a piercingly logical mind, and his words could sting, but his eyes betrayed a mischievous twinkle as he cut to the bone of complex issues with the language of a garage mechanic. A very creative garage mechanic. Nonetheless, his abrasiveness often served a purpose, and he made some early vital connections for me. I recall once painting a watercolor of clouds. I was about nine at the time and Uncle Morris was visiting the house. He walked into my room to look at the painting.

"Do you know what clouds are, Joe?" He called everyone Joe.

"What do you mean?" I responded. "They're things that look like this."

"No," he persisted, "I mean what *are* they, what are they made of?"

"Don't know," I answered, red-faced.

"Then look it up in the encyclopedia," he demanded. "How can you paint something well you don't know about?"

Aesthetic philosophers could have debated with Uncle Morris's hypothesis, but I could not. After having discovered that clouds were just water, I had to admit that the knowledge did make an impact, although I can't say exactly how it affected my painting. What did make a difference was the deep connection he was making for me between seeing and knowing, between art and science, between intuition and information, between seemingly distinct and unconnected areas of thought and perception.

A few years later my parents, Uncle Morris, and I were sitting and chatting in our living room. There was a large radio we were very proud of, an old Capeheart with an arched wooden cabinet, neat knobs and dials and, to my ears, good sound coming out. Classical music, which I loved, was playing, and I was paying no attention to their conversation. Something about that radio suddenly struck me.

"Who made this radio the way it is?" I asked.

"Electrical engineers are responsible for making it work," Uncle Morris responded.

"No, I mean, who is responsible for the whole thing, what it's made out of, the way it looks, the way it *just is?*" I persisted.

"Oh, that, Joe, would be an industrial designer."

He was probably one of the few people in Cleveland, or anywhere, that even knew of the profession at the time. Something about those two very different feeling words, industrial and design, heard together, had immediate resonance for me. Here it was again, that vital link between the physical structure of something and the way it looked. Here was an object, a radio, that brought together all of my passions—it looked great, it worked because of clear, scientific principles, and it was making music.

"That's what I'm going to be when I grow up!" I said. I knew that for a certainty then without knowing anything more about the profession itself.

I have, from those early years, had a fascination with hybrid fields, new disciplines in which previously distinct endeavors blurred their bounds, overlapped, and unlocked unimagined possibilities. Biomechanics, physiological psychology, and of course, medical engineering and industrial design are all built on more than one foundation. As a classical musician in rock and roll, an artist in engineering school, an engineer in art school, and a product designer in automobile design, I have always taken a somewhat perverse pleasure in swimming around in someone else's pond. It has always felt valuable being in a position where I might offer something taken for granted in my own pond, or pick up something no one else thought I needed to know.

Like the fact that clouds are really just water.

8

Intercultural Creativity: Treating Diverse Disciplines as Alien Cultures

We were tired and a bit tense. But we were ready.

The still-tiny staff had worked literally night and day for months to prepare for its first official presentation in Japan. This would be the initial opportunity for Nissan's executives to gauge the value of the new design satellite in distant San Diego, and we were eager to make a strong first impression to reward the support and freedom we had already felt from them.

While the project was somewhat limited in scope (a "facelift," or minor evolutionary change for the 280Z sports car), it would begin to introduce some very foreign forms and graphics into the then-stodgy corporate culture. Every aspect of the presentation had been pored over, from the triple-checked engineering data and accompanying illustrations that approached the level of fine art, to the clay prototype itself, whose pampered surfaces looked for all the world like highly polished steel.

However, this was not a situation where the work could speak for itself. We had been informed that the executives were expecting a formal verbal presentation in addition to all the visual properties we would be bringing, and we were more apprehensive about this than the design itself.

Although Tom Semple, Al Flowers, and I had brought then President Yotsumoto along for guidance, I still felt largely ignorant about Japanese ways, and had yet to start studying the language in earnest. As a result, everything would go through the flattening filter of a translator.

As we gathered the last day before leaving to make sure that everything was in order, I informed the others that I had this great joke to open my introductory remarks, one I thought would surely resonate with the Japanese as much as any American audience. "No, *please*," pleaded Tom and Al in unison, "think of our jobs, our families, our security." We were only months out of Detroit, not yet in our permanent facility, and NDI still felt somewhat unreal and tenuous, almost too good to be true.

"What the hell, guys," I replied. "We need to break the ice. It can't miss." "Let it go, Jerry," continued Tom, "it's just not worth the risk. God knows what cultural taboos you might be breaking."

After quietly listening to this back-and-forth, Mr. Yotsumoto asked, "Hashibag-san, is this your usual way?"

"Yes, generally," I answered. "I like to loosen things up sometimes with a touch of humor at the beginning."

"Then you should just do it," he said flatly, without even asking to hear the joke.

As I entered the presentation room at Nissan's Technical Center, I looked out at what at first struck me as a colony of penguins—black-suited, starch-collared, and ready for business—and experienced a moment of hesitation. But I reassured myself that we had been hired for our differences, and sailed blithely into my opening remarks.

After I told the joke, there wasn't a *flicker* from the audience. Not a trace of discernible reaction. As I paused and scanned the group, waiting for some cue, something off which I might at least bounce a saver, I saw Tom and Al in the back row, heads buried in hands, peering around through their fingers. There was nothing to do but go on, so I proceeded with the presentation.

Afterward, one of the senior executives of Nissan, Mr. Jiro Tanaka, approached me. "We very much appreciated your presentation, Hirshberg-san," he said quietly, with a slight bow.

"*Arigato gozaimasu* (Thanks)," I answered, one of the first phrases I had learned in Japanese.

"And we *particularly* enjoyed your humor," he added.

Mystified, I asked, "Tanaka-san, can you tell me exactly where on a Japanese person I should look next time to detect laughter? You see," I continued, "Western speakers like to establish a certain rhythm with their audience, then sort of play off it."

"Oh," he replied, "we'd never be so personal as to show our teeth during something as important as your first presentation."

"Ah *hah*," I responded.

"But if you want to see Japanese teeth," he continued, grinning now, "just join us for beer and sake this evening."

On my flight back from the presentation, I had the singular and unexpected good fortune of sitting next to Itzhak Perlman, the legendary violinist. We spoke of great music, orchestras, and conductors, and listened to Mahler under our headsets while soaring over the North Pole. The music sent me considerably higher than the thirty-five-thousand-foot altitude of our JAL flight path, and I proceeded to drive him a little crazy with my insistence that he clearly deserved a higher-end audio system (a long-standing interest of mine) than the mediocre one he said he had in his New York apartment.

But more significantly, when I asked him how his performance went in Tokyo, he answered, "I heard it was a great success." Confused, I asked what he meant. "Who could tell?" he responded. "They didn't move, they didn't react, they didn't even *cough* until the end. But then the applause was real and sustained, and the papers raved the next day. So, I guess I did good."

I understood completely. I understood we did not understand. This was for each of us an exposure to real alienness, to a culture marching to a wholly different kind of drummer. Such events— whether playing a concerto, presenting a design, or telling a joke—have proved to be rich occasions for glimpses and insights into the seeming peculiarities of another culture, as well as our own.

We have also discovered that this kind of cross-cultural interaction can lead to some very productive, innovative thinking. This has only happened, however, when we have been willing to dig beneath the surface, to risk exposing our differentness and our ignorance. Stepping out of our own skins and into someone else's is the best way to achieve a heightened awareness of what it means and consciously feels like to be *ourselves*, a state that is difficult to sustain. As it turns out, this elevated cognizance is a key ingredient to creative thought.

***

We knew we had pushed the envelope with the Infiniti J30. Its design took edgeless, fully organic form to the limit, and even violated some sacred design codes. As Tom Semple, the chief designer of the project, and I flew once again to Japan for the final approval of the design, we fully anticipated some resistance. Throughout the long flight, we reassured each other that we had created a potentially significant product.

We were not surprised, therefore, that the reaction to the presentation was mixed and volatile, and that a part of the car caused the Japanese considerable consternation. What *did* take us by surprise was that the most disturbing part of the vehicle to Japanese eyes was the front end.

As Nissan's first luxury car designed specifically for the American market, it would be measured against some of the finest marques in the world, from Germany and England as well as America. Upon assigning us the project, the planners informed us that, no matter how exalted the quality or level of performance, Japan's first luxury cars for this country would lack a critical ingredient common to the competition: classic heritage. So, to make a difficult project even tougher, we were charged with the task of creating a timeless classic, one with instant heritage!

Of course, there is no such thing as "instant heritage" (it is amazing how much double-talk of this kind goes unchallenged in a corporate setting). But we were nevertheless gratified at having been asked to create something new rather than imitate an existing classic. Toyota's approach for its then-new Lexus division was to honor (to put it politely) the imagery of the Mercedes, and while Toyota introduced nothing distinctive of its own, it worked for them economically. Our approach was to study the character of great objects, from chairs to buildings to cars, and then strive to capture their essence in our own way. To our eyes, this essence resided in a clear distinctiveness, a quality of unforced self-confidence, and a sense of stability and balance.

Some of Doug Wilson's early sketches for the vehicle leapt off the wall at us. With just a few strokes he had caught a delicate balance of forms that shouted *classic*. His concept was organized around a sweeping line that ran through the car, beginning low at the leading edge of the hood and front fenders, arching upward through the doors, and descending again on a gently falling deck. It ended at the same height in the rear as it began at the front. This bowed spine was intersected by an ovoid form that defined the coach-like passenger compartment. It is rare for a designer to

149

pinpoint a direction so early in a project, and his sketches served as both a guide and an inspiration throughout the developmental process.

The emergence of the J30 organizing theme, by Doug Wilson

The concept for the J30 was simple and graceful, representing a significant departure from a well-established feature that could be found in virtually all cars on the road at the time. Called the "wedge-form" in the industry, this look was characterized by a high, boxy rear deck sloping down to an aggressively low front end. It had been triggered decades earlier by an aerodynamic principle known as the Kamm effect, used first and most dramatically on sports cars. The application of this principle, discovered by the German aerodynamics scientist Professor Wunibald Kamm, reduces turbulence (and drag) at the rear end of a vehicle by severing the airflow with a high, crisp rear deck configuration.

When the J30 was introduced to the press in America, I

addressed this potentially controversial issue head-on. I referred to the car's unique balance as "challenging the tyranny of the wedge," and the phrase stuck. It was surely this aspect of the new design that we thought would most tax the taste limits of the Japanese.

However, it proved to present no problem to them, as the "falling rear end" had historical antecedents. Many of the great vintage cars, such as the early Delahayes and Jaguars, featured this characteristic. To the Japanese, for whom tradition is a high priority, this striking departure from the current norm was quite acceptable.

The front end, on the other hand, was another story, one about which we were clueless. In our minds it, too, had some classic heritage. A central oval grille on aerodynamically rounded forms flanked by headlights was to be found on many of the great classics. But it was strange, even offensive, to many of the Japanese. Some of the secretaries at the Technical Center, we were told, were made physically ill by the sight of it.

As the presentation was on a Friday, we had the weekend to ponder our problem. Unable to let things go until Monday, Semple and I found a little art supply store near the Royal Park Hotel in Atsugi where we were staying, and for the remainder of the chilly, drizzly weekend, sketched front ends in our tiny rooms.

On Monday, we posted our sketches and gathered some key Japanese individuals for an ad hoc review. Our intent was to cover a wide range of possible "fixes," from subtle adjustments to dramatic changes. We had little hope of actually finding the solution at this meeting, and were trying instead to use the drawings as a means of clarifying the problem.

One of Tom's sketches immediately riveted their attention. It altered the existing design so subtly, I thought at first it was a reference sketch showing the car as it currently was. "This one solves all the problems," said one of the executives. We were flabbergasted. It couldn't be this easy, we thought. None of the adjustments was more than a pencil-line's thickness, yet we had moved from nausea-provoking to acceptable just like that.

We prodded them for an explanation.

"The mouth was frowning," said Mr. Masahisa Koga, a Japanese designer.

"You mean the grille?" I asked, dismayed.

"Yes, the mouth," he responded. The original design featured an asymmetric, elliptical grille with low accents at the corners to flatten its curvature at the bottom and visually anchor it to the bumper. Semple's new sketch raised the corners closer to the centerline of the shape, making the grille symmetrical about its horizontal axis.

"And the eyes looked squinty," added Koga-san.

"The headlamps?" I queried.

"Yes, you've opened them up here. They look less menacing, more trustworthy."

The original design had taken advantage of some new headlamp technology that enabled us to reduce their height. As a result, they appeared as dramatically narrow slots on either side of the grille.

It finally dawned on us. This was no mere front end to the Japanese—it was a face, its headlamps and grille the "eyes" and "mouth," their character and relationship to each other constituting a human expression. Our J30, with its narrowed eyes and nasty, downward-sloping frown, was seen as rude and highly inappropriate. But just as the shift from a frown to a grin is a matter of millimeters on a face, so too was our front transformed from off-putting to appealing with a few minute adjustments that would have no compromising effect on the overall design. Nor would it have any discernible impact on Westerners, for whom fronts of cars were seen primarily as fronts of cars. Had the required changes been of a larger scale, we would have resisted them to preserve the integrity of the design for its intended market.

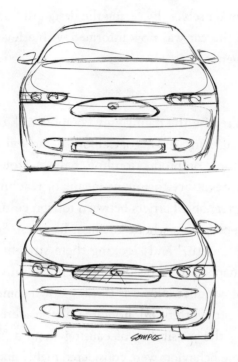

J30 front before and after the dialogue, by Tom Semple

Further discussions stimulated by this discovery led to some surprising realizations. When children in Japan conjure the abstract idea of "car" in their minds, they tend to visualize its front view. And in observing Japanese customers in showrooms or at automobile shows, they generally walk first to the front end to see "who" the car is, unlike Americans and Europeans, who go first to the side, circle it once, kick the tires, and then get inside.

Clearly, it was not possible to assume that a product would convey a consistent meaning from one country to another, nor was it possible to anticipate the ways it would be perceived. Our design had generated some unexpected and unintended reactions in a foreign milieu, and we had been given the opportunity to fix the perceived problem ourselves. By seeing the design through the eyes of the Japanese, the car was now informed with a level of international "intelligence."

* * *

In order to realize the dauntingly complex task of conceiving automobile designs in San Diego, California, and seeing them faithfully manufactured on production lines halfway around the world, NDI found it necessary to invent means of reaching across the seemingly impregnable barriers between foreign cultures. We were dealing with a people for whom "saying it like it is," "going directly to the horse's mouth," and "looking them straight in the eyes" (even if they happen to be headlamps) were not universally recognized codes of conduct. Nor was turning down someone's urgent request with a straightforward, honest "no" considered more noble than avoiding the possibility of causing them a "loss of face." Indeed, all these behaviors were considered highly unappealing and even untrustworthy by the Japanese. But over time, by struggling to remain open and dispassionate during discordant dealings, we learned not only how to read the myriad shadings (and ways of expressing) "yes" and "no" in Japan, but also how to grasp the very different roles these words play for each of us.

Mutual understanding of any issue, no matter how small, was never taken for granted. Through a process focused on patient, nonjudgmental observation and questioning, those deep, unspoken assumptions and underlying values rarely broached within a single culture were exposed and examined between the Japanese and the Americans.

It was, of course, far easier said than done. Maintaining patience and neutrality during moments of mutual tension and deep misunderstanding was not easy, and we often failed. Nor has this been the popularly sanctioned approach for dealing with other cultures. Our presidents and statespersons are judged primarily for their toughness abroad, for their ability to "hammer out" agreements, to "ram through" Washington's positions, to "stand their ground" and "prevail." While graduate schools encourage the learning of some basic international cordialities and a few no-nos, the deeper, touchier issues are deemed out of bounds, off-base, and generally unwise to engage. Creative resolutions are therefore seldom achieved.

Surely, such subjects as World War II or current attitudes in Japan regarding the Jews would be considered out-of-bounds topics in business relationships. Every paperback I've read on doing business with the Japanese urges sticking to the weather when not talking business. But after spending some time together, we have learned it is not only possible but necessary to occasionally discuss the most awkward of issues, not just to break the ice but to try to understand each other's racial and national underpinnings. And we have found that even the Japanese, with their reputed levels of courtesy and respect for privacy, are equally willing to get beneath the surface to examine our own areas of vulnerability: the prevalence of violence and crime, the falling standards of culture and education, and rising levels of weight. While such discussions can at times be unsettling and possibly even threatening, they can also become trip wires for fresh takes on old assumptions. In other words, they are opportunities for new ideas.

Since our creative output had been high right from the start, it was becoming apparent to me that something about this struggle to understand and be understood by an alien culture was energizing to our imaginations. We began to focus on our differences, working to find ways to more fully hear and be heard, see and be seen. There seemed to be no end to the discoveries that were possible on a daily basis, and the vast gaps between us were turned into fertile, imaginative space as long as we were willing to fully immerse ourselves in this undefined, shifting, and vaguely ominous region.

❊❊❊

Certainly, two distinct languages provided plenty of space for both confusion and discovery. While we found ways to communicate with almost no common words between us, I wanted to learn Japanese almost from the beginning of this venture. It was at once sobering and embarrassing to encounter dispatch after Japanese dispatch capable of at least rudimentary communication in my own tongue, and even more humbling when a flock of giggling, uniformed schoolkids passed me on the street in Kyoto trying out "Haro, meestah! (Hello, mister)." Furthermore, negotiating with a people who knew my language without my knowing theirs seemed a weak starting position, and I wanted to play on a more level communications field.

I first approached the daunting task of learning Japanese in much the same way I might for a different system of monetary exchange. I remembered my first study of a second language, Hebrew, as merely a Bar Mitzvah requirement; and my second, Spanish, as merely a school requirement—vocabulary, grammar, conjugation, and more vocabulary.

My tutor has told me I am now operating somewhere around the level of a sixth grader, although I suspect some generosity in her assessment. Aside from the evident delight the Japanese take in seeing anyone make a serious attempt beyond the Berlitz-level approach, I have been amazed at the complex, *nonverbal* layers of their culture that have been revealed to me through this primarily verbal study. As it turns out, these dimensions are difficult to access in any other way.

I make no pretense at expertise in linguistic analysis, but cannot help noting some of the ways that thinking in another language has enabled me to regard the world. In order to benefit from the rich rewards of speaking a second language, it is necessary to move beyond the mechanics of a system of communication, and contemplate its overall design, tone weight, rhythm, and texture; its inherent logic and accepted areas of irrationality, as well as what it reveals about an utterly different way of organizing and processing the world to which it refers.

For example, realizing the Japanese do not always conjugate for singular or plural seems completely consonant with the manner in which they think and behave. If someone says, "I will be bringing dog with me to dinner tomorrow," do not be surprised if they bring ten. (They seldom use articles.) Much of the information communicated in Japan resides in specific contexts, and they are very proud of the "context-rich" nature of their discourse. The lack of clear distinction between the individual and the group in their syntax has helped me to see how dramatically we emphasize this distinction in the very structure of our own language, as well as in our behavior.

Asking for a personal opinion of a Japanese individual can cause obvious discomfort, and typically yields a response related to a plurality, a reflection on the prevailing opinion of a certain group toward a subject. To Americans, this is mere conformism. To the Japanese, for whom conformity is not necessarily negative, the difficulty of expressing an individual point of view is embedded in the language and the ethos. It no longer drives me quite so crazy when, upon being confronted with an object as inspiring as a shiny new full-size car prototype, a group of Japanese stand stone-silent. Rather than expect a spontaneous response, American-style, I now understand that one will be forthcoming, but only after the individual/group composite reaction has been consensualized. While dissenting opinions will still be held, they will be expressed only in the context of the community. From the Japanese mind-set, our immediate, individual reactions can appear hasty, brash, and ill-considered; from our point of view, theirs can seem compromised, hesitant, and overconsidered.

But while the group is all-important in Japan, the language is saturated with words and phrases and communication structures to honor and protect the individual. There are myriad verbal softeners and qualifiers that cushion the listener from forthcoming remarks that might otherwise be offensive or too direct. I will never learn the countless ways of saying "excuse me, but . . ." or "I'm sorry that . . ." or "please accept by abruptness, however . . ." Because of this way of communicating, many have mistakenly assumed that the Japanese never say "no." Actually, they do, but so subtly we tend to miss it. In response to an invitation, an American might typically respond, "No, I won't be going with you tomorrow." The "no" is right up front. A direct translation of the same response from the Japanese is, "As to my going with you tomorrow, it's no." The "no" occurs at the very end of the sentence and is buffered by lots of neutral words before it, sort of verbal bumpers to diffuse the negativity. It is extremely difficult to be blunt, to "come on strong" and still speak correct Japanese. Which is not to say that the Japanese cannot say what must be said or do what must be done. If your head must come off, it will. Courteously.

Our understanding of this characteristic played a central role in conceiving the unique interior design of the Cocoon, the concept vehicle mentioned earlier, for the Tokyo International Automobile Show. In formulating the design, NDI was asked to consider the growing trend of three generations of families living in one household due to the astronomical costs of real estate in Japan.

As the car would have to seat six (virtually everyone limits themselves to two kids in Japan), the parents, grandparents, and children were arranged in three rows of two seats. Each seating area was treated as a zone of architecturally implied semi-isolation. But as with the language itself, it was done subtly, with a kind of courteous form-vocabulary. The seats were bowl-shaped and engulfing. The roofline continued this encapsulating motif with six slightly concave and softly lit cavities over each seating position. And a gently undulating center console ran the full length of the interior, further dividing the region and providing creature comforts located for easy reach from each orb. It was as though there was an invisible sphere carving out a comfortable cocoon for each passenger. While there were no actual privacy barriers, we knew these architectural bubbles of space would be honored as personal territories in Japan. Furthermore, we realized that this idea, one that grew from an immersion in a foreign mind-set, might work nicely for commuter cars and other vehicles in America or Europe requiring a sense of implied privacy, such as train and airplane interiors.

*** *** ***

When considering Dana Borgatti for a modeling position, we had no qualms about his character or talent. But there was concern about the challenges of communicating across a difficult language barrier, as he spoke very little of our language. Speaking about visual form with words requires one difficult layer of translation, and adding yet another language into the transaction seemed fraught with potential for miscommunication. But we were impressed with his enthusiasm and ability, and decided to hire him, convinced we could work things out.

We found a language tutor and, on a voluntary basis, invited anyone interested to participate. To our delight, there was nearly one hundred percent involvement. Although only a few became proficient, the common language between Dana and the staff grew, and through his patience and our stumbling efforts, he became a significant contributor to the creative team.

Of equal importance, those involved directly with him on a project have reaped an unexpected bonus. In the not-always-successful attempt to find a means of expressing an idea (especially one not yet fully formed) with a severely limited vocabulary, they were inevitably left with a sharper grasp of their *own* thoughts. In the process of distilling an idea down to its essence, considerable clarity was gained. And everyone became painfully aware of how inefficiently we communicate with each other in a common tongue.

Dana Borgatti's language is signing. He has been deaf since early childhood, but has helped us all to hear better.

***

There are, of course, many other dimensions of cultural expression beyond language that NDI struggles with, learns from, and observes: the different distances we regard as appropriate during ordinary conversation; the proper speaking volumes and even pitch levels; the issues of time, as in what constitutes an appropriate workday or even what it means to be on time or late; and even the very different tastes and tolerances for aromas. It is certainly possible to err and overgeneralize about each of these. However, to ignore them is to miss opportunities for deeper mutual understanding, keener self-awareness, and the kind of fresh orientation that leads to new ideas.

The interaction of two alien cultures clearly held great potential for inspiring unexpected directions, such as the Infiniti J30 front end revisions and the Cocoon concept vehicle. And the effort to deal with the complex language and cultural issues had proven helpful in developing our skills at working with a foreign people. We were not, however, doing so well between the exceptionally diverse individuals and departments we had assembled within NDI's *own* culture.

I began wondering if we might be making some of the same kinds of false assumptions about each other as we had with the Japanese. The success of our intercultural efforts and their surprising impact on our creative energies led to the startling notion of treating each specialized discipline within the same culture as an "alien" culture, one with its own language, education, goal-orientation, and history.

It is not easy to know how or where to step outside your own culture, your own skin. Here, everything is simply as it has been. Just as I can no longer hear the omnipresent tone of D at which the electric current continually hums at work, or without considerable effort, detect the complex aromas that characterize my own home, so too have we ceased being aware of the very specific, one-off ways we Americans exist in the world.

In some ways, the gap between distinct departments and professions within the same culture is even more difficult to bridge than that between two countries, as everyone assumes that common appearances mean shared values and perspectives. Beneath the surface, however, the ways of being in the world, the very meaning of success or failure, and even the languages spoken by marketing, finance, engineering, sales, and design are as alien to one another as those of foreign nationalities.

The challenge was to distance myself from the various individual personalities at NDI in order to gain the clarity I had experienced in working with the Japanese—and to discover and best utilize the creative opportunities lying hidden in the differences among us. We opted for the insight provided by various applications of psychology to organizational design and business.

***

Ron Reneau, an organizational behavior consultant we had contracted, characterized me as someone who, when confronted by an appealing vista, was likely to dive off the cliff on an impulse, yelling up from halfway down, "Let's build a parachute, *now!*" When he voiced this notion at a meeting of our top managers, I chuckled at the characterization, but many present found it not the least bit amusing. Most of these were engineers, administrators, shop personnel, and modelers, those whose task in the company was the conceiving, paying for, and building of such parachutes for some of the more impulsive designers. My frustration with what I perceived as their resistance to making creative leaps was what had led to contracting the consultant in the first place.

When I had earlier experienced a similar sense of alienation from the Japanese, I confronted them with a truly blank, uncomprehending mind. And the questions I asked were, at first, embarrassingly basic and naive-sounding. But the answers, while utterly foreign to my own way of being in the world, were wonderfully elucidating. Grasping the rationale behind the reasons, absorbing the bedrock of cultural priorities and values, clarified what previously had been mysterious, frustrating, and at times even frightening. When confronting crossed signals with someone in my own culture, however, I passed them off largely as personality conflicts, and seldom bothered to ask the question why. I became determined to clear my mind of all assumptions about the values and personal starting points of my fellow Americans.

After the meeting, I awkwardly asked a cross-section of attendees about my "cliff-diving" management style, craving a fuller understanding of its impact. But the responses were all over the map, and I felt at a loss. After spending further time with us, Reneau suggested the use of a psychological instrument called Personalysis. While similar to other personality-mapping devices in its identification of four primary behavioral dimensions, this one was especially appealing to NDI as it presented its findings visually in four primary colors. After everyone completed a questionnaire, the results were represented on a quadrant displaying varying quantities of red, blue, yellow, and green. These colors indicated our preferred ways of managing ourselves and being managed, and revealed those basic needs that had to be met in order for each of us to function effectively. There were further dimensions to be perceived from the specific clusters of colors predominant in our maps. And there were two inarguable givens: the colors didn't change, and there were no good or bad colors.

"Red people" were the doers. They were happiest when making evident progress, least happy when anything impeded their sense of forward movement. And when unhappy, "reds" let you know about it, directly.

"Yellows" were the people people. Not needing to be out front, they were happiest supporting and enabling the group and needed only to be included. *Not* being invited to participate sent them into deep stress, and even in that state they would not be alone. They would bring the town down with them.

"Greens" were down to earth and sticklers for detail. They could (and had to) actually balance their checkbooks, a source of constant amazement to me. They were grounded, and wanted above all to be accountable. "Greens" knew the facts and the rules, and they disliked surprises. When things seemed vague or were not thoroughly considered, they became unhappy. And when a green was unhappy, it was wise to find a lawyer. Quickly.

Blue was the predominant NDI color. It was the color of thought, as in "blue sky," or ideas, as in "out of the blue." "Blues" needed two things above all: to understand and to be understood. When they were not, they sulked (as in "getting the blues") and wanted to be alone, preferably on some remote island.

These colors provided a one-dimensional snapshot of our personas, how we liked to relate, and be related to. A serial murderer and a bassoonist could have identical hues, and there would be no correlation between any set of shades and either success or failure. This very simplicity made the instrument useful in clarifying unexpectedly tangled or hurtful encounters by focusing attention on the ways someone *else* preferred being dealt with.

It seemed awkward at first to ask Larry Brinker, director of modeling and the individual responsible for setting up NDI's entire model-making capability, about his core priority at work or, for that matter, in life. After all, I had observed and worked closely with him not only at NDI but during much of my time at GM. I hired him not only for his sculptural talent, but for his vast understanding about how things worked. He was the consummate handyman on a grand scale. When complimented on his new home built on a small mountaintop in rural Ramona, he'd reply, in his still-detectable Indiana drawl, "Yeah, thanks, I built the dang thing"—and he meant it in a way most people who used the phrase did not. What he meant was, he bought the machine to dig the hole, poured the concrete, laid the plumbing, nailed the frame, insulated, glazed, wired, and roofed it . . . himself.

So he seemed to me the right person to build up the composite of hardwares (clay ovens, steel platforms, accurate measuring and cutting devices, tools, computer linkups with Japan, etc.) and establish the procedures and levels of both technical and artistic skill required to put together objects even more complex than homes: automobiles. Over the years, he has assembled a formidable cast of modelers and prototype makers. "You're in the big leagues now," said one proud veteran recently to a wide-eyed newcomer. Brinker created a concept-realization department as fine as any in the world.

But Larry was one of the visibly unamused individuals present at those meetings when I, without prior warning, "jumped off the cliff." Not only was he not inspired by my enthusiastic impulses, he was genuinely concerned and deeply stressed.

"We've come up with a whole new twist for the car developing in Blue Studio," I announced midway through a project at a hastily called meeting of the chiefs. "It's very new, a big improvement, very exciting and . . ."

"Very late!" interjected Brinker.

"I know, Lar," I continued, exasperated at this characteristic response, "but we've got to go for it."

"Sure, we can do it," he added, "but, of course, all work in the other studios will have to stop. And we'll probably have to go on a full overtime schedule for the next two months. Other than that, no problem."

Tension between us at such moments was palpable and *not* creatively abrasive. From my perspective—as well as the perspective of those designers responsible for the new directions—Brinker seemed resistant to creative leaps, too "bound by the book." Ideas, after all, came when they came and the question at NDI shouldn't have been *whether* to execute them, but how. From his vantage point, and that of many others responsible for such things as the schedule, the cost, the accuracy, and the physical act of actually doing the prototyping, this tendency to make apparently willy-nilly changes in direction midstream was ill considered, inefficient, and potentially dangerous to the overall quality of our output.

I had reached a point of considerable befuddlement and frustration before finally realizing I really did not know who Larry Brinker was. Seeing his Personalysis chart for the first time was something of a revelation. Not that I was surprised at his colors, but seeing the picture created by his particular mix of hues in contrast to my own helped me to see him with fresh eyes. His chart was dominated by green, with a strong dollop of red as well. Mine was dominated by blue, with significant amounts of red and yellow. As to green, I was told I may have set the all-time record for scoring virtually none. Translation: Brinker would, above all else in life, need to feel accountable. He would need to get from here to there, but only after crafting a clear, reliable plan. I, on the other hand, would jump off cliffs, leaving a hopelessly out-of-balance checkbook behind.

If accountability represented the very breath of his life, I had unknowingly been knocking the wind out of him from the beginning. With a better understanding of his priorities and needs at our disposal, possible remedies to our situation began to emerge.

I still leap off cliffs, but when the impulse strikes, I pause to notify Brinker that a change of direction is being considered, that there will be a meeting to discuss it soon, and that I'd like to hear everything about it that concerns him. When the meeting occurs, I generally ask to hear the bad news first. For Brinker, having some time to mull it over reduces the element of surprise. And knowing there will be an audience for his concerns eliminates the potential for him to have to assume the unwanted "bad-guy" role.

Naturally, my interest in his concerns cannot be disingenuous. Identifying the aliens among us is not a process of manipulation, of pushing the right buttons to get whatever you want. What is achieved in recognizing our differences is the equivalent of learning a foreign language—the subtleties are often more telling than the words themselves.

Like the engineers, administrators, modelers, shop personnel, and even some of the designers whose green buttons I had been inadvertently pushing, Larry Brinker showed a dramatic increase in his contributions to and support of the creative effort. He has since conceived of countless ingenious devices, tools, and new methodologies for NDI. He has further developed his own unique theories of form that he enjoys sharing with NDI's modeling staff, along with students at the Rhode Island School of Design, where he has become a regular lecturer. Yet, he is still accurate, thorough, and unconditionally responsible. And for the cliff-jumpers at NDI, it was wonderfully comforting to learn that our parachute-builders held accountability as their highest priority and deepest need.

Everyone at NDI displays the little plastic "color maps" in their work areas for all to see. When creative differences or interpersonal problems arise, the maps are often consulted in discussions. Whenever we hire new people, they are given their "colors" by members of the staff, who readily share their own. And in spite of the fact that the Personalysis test is in English, it has proven surprisingly accurate across national boundaries.

* * *

Personalysis is but one of many means we utilize to tap into the energies of our mutual alienness. Recently, while meeting to reconsider and further refine our personnel evaluation forms, someone came up with the novel idea of instituting a self-evaluation process for the groups we're constantly forming at NDI. After all, we are continually experimenting with assembling new teams, and needed an opportunity for the team members to reflect upon and express what was working and what was not.

Although the notion had immediate appeal, we knew that, given the difficulties we had faced in identifying a meaningful tool for individual appraisal, we would surely need some professional assistance in evaluating group performance. NDI has enjoyed an ongoing relationship with Dr. Stan Fevens, a Canadian organizational psychologist around whom turbulence inevitably seems to subside. Originally called in to help us grow our leadership capabilities (not a high priority among our hiring considerations), he gradually became embroiled in various levels of the operation. Like a big, weather-worn ship working its way through the roiling waters, Dr. Fevens always took his time, which seemed to leave us more of it.

With his innate grasp of the creative process, he was not resistant to helping us develop an approach quite unlike any he had used before. He actually seemed to prefer it when we groped to find our own means of reaching psychological insight, clumsy as it might at first have been.

It eventually became customary to gather for group evaluations at the conclusion of each project, although anyone could pull the cord on the train at any point to call for a session. The atmosphere for these assessments, with Fevens' help, was dedicated to honest, heartfelt expression without devolving into painful "sensitivity sessions." Rather than asking for mutual criticisms, for example, everyone instead was to think in terms of what they wanted another individual or group to continue, stop, or start doing. And it worked.

The procedure has effectively illuminated issues that did not arise from the individual-oriented personnel evaluations. What we found was that large, unsuspected gaps continued to exist between collaborating departments. Even after the completion of projects deemed highly successful from the executive point of view, we were continually surprised at the degree to which one or another of the participating disciplines felt short-circuited, unheard, or otherwise impeded in their efforts to contribute as effectively as they might. This self-evaluation procedure further sensitized us to the very foreign ways each group approached its work and even defined success. We were getting better at identifying the alien among us, and it was *us*.

Our discussions at these continuing forums are not necessarily heavy, hurtful, or heated. We try to be hard on the issues, soft on the people. Often, the sessions offer opportunities to retrace the history of the task and celebrate the experience. We have found it just as meaningful (and challenging) to try to learn from what we happened to do *right* as what we did wrong, something most companies do not spend enough time doing. And not least, the very act of bringing the diverse groups back together for an appraisal of their performance has helped to identify them as teams of compatriots with a vested interest in working out their differences.

It is, of course, not the intention of group self-evaluations to promote sameness. Differences in style and approach are not only *not* ironed out, they are sharpened and thrown into high relief. The idea is to recognize and more fully utilize those differences and the critical balance of skills and approaches they represent.

And just as with our attempts to bridge the gaps with the Japanese, language again emerged as one of the key hurdles, even though this time we were all ostensibly speaking the same one. As the British have famously said about their relations with America, our corporation turned out to comprise many cultures separated by a common language. In truth, professional dialects are as diverse and mutually incomprehensible as Brooklynese, Malibuese, or Alabamese. The problem is, the differences are far subtler and seem less urgent than those between national foreign tongues. Yet, even the multiple meanings of apparently simple words can lead to periods of confusion and, more dangerously, false assumptions of shared agreement.

When visiting the Cal Tech wind tunnel not long ago, a group of fluid-dynamics engineers and designers from NDI agreed on the importance of the accuracy and quality of the model in aerodynamic evaluations. It took quite some time before we all realized, with considerable embarrassment, that when using the term "model," the designers had been referring to something tangible made of clay, plastic, and wood, while the engineers were addressing a mathematical analogue related to the science of fluid dynamics. I was amazed at how long we were able to discuss the subject with seeming coherence before realizing we were not connecting at all.

Yet, at a deeper level, what we were talking about did indeed make sense. Each of our models functioned as both analogue and physical representation of "the real thing." Since the NDI designers prefer to make the necessary adjustments required for aerodynamic efficiency to the forms of a real, three-dimensional model—and the engineers find it far easier to simply alter their virtual forms on the computer terminal—we began to ponder some new and more efficient ways of relating and integrating these two distinct models of reality. We had to trip over this option to see it, and then had to be willing to think about the different meanings and connotations of the word "model" even though we were speaking the same language. In reconsidering what was presumed a commonly understood word, the way was cleared for some unexpected and novel opportunities.

With multidisciplinary teams, language clearly cannot be taken for granted. The potential for misunderstanding as well as inspiration exists everywhere, not only *between* words but *within* them.

***

Many of the strategies for fostering creativity are mechanisms for jarring us loose from our moorings, for rethinking the ways we formulate our environment, assumptions, or relationships. But once it is accepted that a common language and orientation between disciplines is not nearly so common as has been thought, it becomes necessary to assume nothing and to risk asking all the embarrassingly obvious questions. When this is done, the various disciplines and departments within a company begin to feel more fully understood, their values, goals, idiosyncracies, and languages honored in a way usually reserved for foreigners.

For *the creative priority*, this is truly model behavior.

9

Drinking from Diverse Wells

"Istanbul, Jerry," called Yvette.

"Right."

"Really, it is."

"Yes, and I'm Bond, James Bond."

"Jerry," lowering her voice a semitone, "Istanbul is on the line."

Yvette Prado is my executive assistant and vital extra limb. By now she knows exactly how to gather my full attention when necessary with only the subtlest shifts in emphasis and tone.

"It's about some kind of yacht," she continued.

It sounded like the setup for a massive practical joke, which idea was only reinforced by the in-the-next-room clarity of the voice on the phone, one that surely should have been badly distorted coming from such an exotic location. Even more startling was the nearly flawless, uninflected English of Dr. Ekber Onuk, the vigorous president of Yonca Teknik, a Turkish shipbuilding company.

NDI has been extraordinarily fortunate in the character of its nonautomotive clients. Since we announced at start-up that we

were available for general product design work, certain kinds of corporate executives have found their way to us, risk-accommodating
individuals undaunted by the notion of going outside their areas of
expertise for input and collaboration. This self-selecting group is
not only drawn to the fresh take a group of outsiders might bring,
but eager to depart from the existing norms in their fields. And this
was precisely the kind of work in which we wanted to engage to
stretch our creative muscles.

With energetic enthusiasm for his product, Dr. Onuk proceeded
to tell me about an amazing new hull configuration conceived by a
noted Swiss hydroengineer, Erbil Serter, that represented a significant breakthrough in fluid dynamics. Thin as a fin and lower in the
water at the prow than the stern, it enabled a vessel to cut through
the waves with virtually no drag or whitewater.

He had a wealthy client ready to support the first application of
this principle to a hundred-and-five-foot luxury yacht. It would
boast a one-piece, Kevlar and S-glass–composite (essentially an
extremely strong yet light form of Fiberglas) hull, sleep twenty-five,
and be powered by an impressive five-thousand-horsepower aircraft
turbine flanked by German-made twin diesel MTUs. Furthermore,
there were plans at the time for this superyacht to attempt a world
record and attain the coveted Blue Ribbon Prize by crossing the
Atlantic in under forty hours without refueling, which meant attaining speeds in excess of eighty knots, or over ninety miles per hour!

Yes, Yvette, it was indeed about some kind of yacht. Here was a
project to take us into truly foreign waters.

Yonca had first gone to an established Italian boat design group
and had been disappointed at the results (which we asked not to
see). "Since this was truly breakthrough technology," Onuk
explained, "we wanted a truly breakthrough design to express it.
What we got from the Italians was stunning but mainstream, not
reflective of the departure this concept represents."

Dr. Onuk happened to be as passionate about cars as boats, and also as informed. He had followed NDI's history and was familiar with both our products and our philosophy. Even though I knew that some of our products were sold in that part of the world, this was amazing to me. "I purchased one of the first Pathfinders in Turkey," he said, "and am attracted to the way NDI fuses art and technology.

"Do you do boats?" he asked finally.

"On Thursdays," I responded cryptically, trying to conceal my eagerness.

We had an instant rapport, and the project was launched. While a few of us at NDI had actually worked with boats, none of us possessed anything resembling expertise. NDI was to be responsible for everything from the chine line (essentially the water line) up. Artline, the world's leading boat interior design group from Arnhelm, the Netherlands, would be doing the ship's living and sleeping quarters. This firm had earlier done the interior of the famed Moonraker, named after the James Bond film. It was the former record holder as the world's fastest yacht. To complete his team, Onuk had selected the highly respected naval architectural company Sharp/DeFever. As it turned out, they were located along the bay in San Diego which, at the time, was home to the Americas Cup Trophy and a hotbed of leading-edge shipbuilding know-how.

The market for which we would be designing was worlds away from anything we had yet encountered. On the one hand, these superyachts were recreational and status toys for the wealthiest of the wealthy (our sloop was in the ten-million-dollar range). Achieving world records with these boats was, from the perspective of their owners, for the sole purpose of temporary bragging rights at the world's most elite harbors. Indeed, we were to pay particular attention to the stern of the boat, as it would spend most of its time backed into slips at places such as Monte Carlo and Saint-Tropez. When asked where in America we might go to see yachts in this class, Onuk reticently informed us that finding any here would be highly unlikely, with the possible exception of a few in Miami.

On the other hand, just as in car racing, this is a region of business where experiments with untried technologies and risky new directions are both encouraged and supported. In order to earn those highly prized bragging rights, the wealthy enthusiasts find the entrepreneurs, who in turn find (or are found by) the inventors and creators.

Of course, luxury yachts capable of such levels of performance are taken to their limits about as often as sport utility vehicles are driven off-road. "It's quite unpleasant," explained Onuk with characteristic understatement. "Actually crossing an ocean at these speeds for sustained periods of time is usually a one-time-only event." Knowing my own level of seaworthiness, I turned down the opportunity of going on the maiden voyage, becoming queasy at the very thought of it.

Since the boat would be capable of such significant speeds, we immediately saw it as a vessel needing to be fluid and efficient while moving simultaneously through water *and* air. The unique hull took care of the water, and with our extensive experience in aerodynamics, we found it quite natural to develop efficient forms for the upper surfaces of the boat that included such drag-reducing automotive technologies as flush-glass systems.

While a team including Bruce Campbell, Alfonso Albaisa, Doug Wilson, Larry Brinker, and I worked the exterior forms, Al Flowers focused on the critical design of the helm stations, wanting to effect a dramatic sense of location and the feeling of a pilot's cockpit. Without the more intimate, enveloping scale of automotive architecture relative to the human body, this was a unique challenge for a car designer.

Indeed, it was the sheer scale both inside and out that presented the greatest challenge to us. Up to that point, the car was, by a significant margin, the largest object with which we had ever dealt. Most designers never have to design anything as large as an automobile, which was less than one-fifth the scale of this yacht. The expressive impact of such design elements as subtly rising, falling and curving lines, or of slightly convex or concave surfaces, were magnified many times over at these dimensions. This was not an object we could easily get our visual arms around, let alone grasp by walking around it. We had not only to use different lenses, but to develop a whole new set of aesthetic sensibilities.

This work was carried out at NDI not by a separate group of designers and modelers in a partitioned, nonautomotive studio. That would have defeated the underlying purpose of the activity itself, one highly unique among car design studios in America and rare throughout the world. We worked ongoing automotive assignments and the Yonca project side by side, boat models emerging next to car models, land-bound and oceangoing concept sketches crowding each other on the same sheets of paper.

Dealing with two challenging products, one for the land and one for the sea, could at times become overwhelming. But there was something about becoming simultaneously immersed and even lost in apparently unrelated tasks that held the promise of leading us to unexpected places. While there was no conscious attempt to cross-pollinate forms, technologies, or concepts between the projects, we knew that the likelihood of juxtaposed thinking was enormously enhanced in such circumstances.

A striking direction for the yacht penned by Alfonso Albaisa was eventually selected. It featured a powerful, singular sweep of organically integrated form, one that surely would have caused the villains on any of the exotic boats in the Bond films to take a serious look. With its fully integrated panels of black-tinted flush glass, the vessel looked as capable of flight as it did of submerging itself smoothly underwater if necessary. Having worked closely with Ekber Onuk, Doug Sharp at Sharp/DeFever, and the interior designers at Art-line, we came up with a design that met all functional requirements, and the shipbuilders in Istanbul were able to follow our plans to a T.

Above: original scale model of the YONtech 105. Below: actual ship on its maiden voyage in the Black Sea

Al Flowers' design for the helm station was equally well received. By skillfully shaping the captain's chair, control panel, and surrounding surfaces in relation to one another, he was able to fashion an implied shell around the pilot and to evoke a strong sense of place in a semi-open, vast, and otherwise undifferentiated space.

Although the secondary gain of creative impetus from such outside projects was most often subliminal, there were instances of demonstrable cross-fertilization. Flowers' helm station was one of them. It provided the inspiration for the interior of the Cocoon three-generation sedan discussed in Chapter 8. The experience gained in creating a virtual bubble of space on the deck of a ship startlingly transferred itself to the very different but associated use of suggesting several cocoons of implied privacy for a multiple family car.

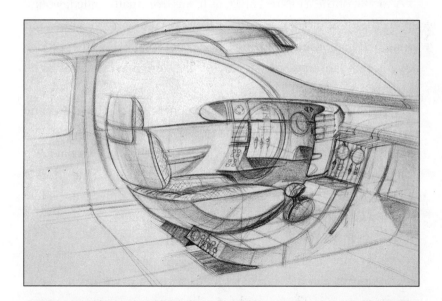

Concept sketch of the Helm station by Al Flowers, and the interior design of the Cocoon, to which it led

Of even greater import to the staff was the mental stretch we experienced working on an object of this grand scale. The project necessitated thinking about such fundamental issues as a car's scale, something we had come to take for granted, and forced us to deal with it anew. In our now considerably enlarged frame of reference, the automobile suddenly seemed quite modest and manageable in size. Sensitivities and skills gained from having worked with forms of this magnitude gave NDI some unique advantages over most car design studios limiting themselves to working on only one product and at one scale.

A model of the YONtech 105, as it was eventually called, wound up on the desk of then-president Ozu of Turkey, with whose son Onuk had had business dealings. It was not long before the Turkish navy became interested in deploying the design as a fleet of naval patrol boats.

Naturally, we cannot take *all* assignments that come our way, no matter how interesting. When offered the opportunity of converting the helm station to a gunnery turret for the Turkish navy, we politely declined, having grown fond of our kneecaps. This, in spite of Doug Wilson's fervent pleas to accept the assignment, as he had been drawing naval cannons since he had been eight.

***

Concentrated work tends to focus attention within an ever-narrowing region. This inward-funneling effect is, of course, necessary, not only to the mastery of an area of expertise but to the creative process as well. However, just as creativity requires periodic distancing, work, too, benefits from periods of unfocusing and refocusing.

Management tends to concern itself with the full and continuous concentration of the staff on the work at hand, believing that the most reliable way to get from here to there is to "keep your eye on the ball." The problem is, after a while, it is no longer possible to really see the ball for what it is, let alone assess the playing field, or imagine what lies beyond it that might prove useful to the task at hand.

In fact, it requires greater effort to encourage periods of disengagement and to direct attention *away* from a primary activity once it has become the center of focus. Work has its own gravitational field, and the intervention of skilled leadership can help in occasionally pulling away from it. This, however, is a counterintuitive move, one that can appear (and even feel) irresponsible and inefficient to those not directly involved.

Disengaging from an involving task, one with which we are not yet finished, does not amount to abandoning it. Quite the contrary. While conscious focus shifts elsewhere, the subconscious continues grinding away, considering anything that comes its way as grist for the mill. And that grist, defined as anything than can be turned to an advantage, might be found almost anywhere. Our preoccupied minds will mine any new activity, sifting continually through it for previously unseen connections, for bits and parts to fill the nagging void of an unfinished, unresolved question.

***

Flying home from a talk I had given in Palo Alto, California, I was fully immersed in sketching around a problem area of the Infiniti J30, oblivious to the person sitting next to me. He thoughtfully waited until I looked up from the drawings and began to rub some life back into my eyes, before engaging me in conversation.

"Are you by any chance Jerry Hirshberg?" he asked.

"How on earth did you know that?" I responded, surprised.

"Not too many folks returning to San Diego can draw cars like that," he observed.

I could not, however, have guessed who Rick Shrameck was. Casually dressed and with an easy manner, he did not strike me as a hard-driving entrepreneur in the mushrooming field of computer technology. His quick, alert eyes and the heady pace of our conversation should have been clues, however. We spoke of cars, about which he knew quite a lot, and computers, about which I knew very little. Upon disembarking in San Diego, we shook hands, agreeing that NDI would be taking a crack at the industrial design for his latest computer concept.

Rick Shrameck, the CEO of RDI Computer Corporation at the time, was in the business of conceptualizing new categories of computers, hardware packages selected and arranged for new sets of uses. He had a strong team of engineers and computer scientists, and a network of prototyping and manufacturing contacts that extended to Europe and the Far East. Like the founders of Apple, he also had a unique appreciation of the role of design for this user-intensive product. Unlike most hardware developers, however, he did not feel bound by the numbing conformity of virtually all computer design at the time, a sea of beige, rectangular boxes.

He had contrived the notion of a powerful, portable workstation, something between a permanent terminal at the office and a fully mobile laptop, by utilizing the (then) newly emerging efficiencies of RISC-chip technology. With a projected weight of about ten pounds and the size of a briefcase, it would be a bit bulky for a plane but easy to take home for an evening or weekend. And it had more byte-crunching capability than the full-size workstations we were then using in the administration department of NDI.

Schrameck was concerned about the growing lack of "desktop real estate" in the emerging office, one that was clearly not going to be the paperless world Bill Gates and others had imagined. While not aiming for a smaller screen or keypad, however, he wanted a device "with the smallest possible footprint." And so we conceived of a screen that would be modular and easily detachable. We imagined situations where it might be hung on a nearby wall, thereby not only reducing the computer's bulk, but providing a physical environment for easy collaboration and presentation possibilities.

With Europe as the principally targeted market for the product, he wanted "a statement," even "a work of art." And he envisioned a friendlier, more fluid and welcoming form-vocabulary than the intelligent-looking but cool and edgy crispness of most existing designs. This was, after all, "a product people are literally in touch with for the better part of their workdays," he said.

This time, the challenge for a group of car designers was in focusing down. Here was a product and a body of concerns at the other end of the dimensional scale. The car, which was less than one-fifth the size of a boat, was more than five times the size of this computer. Fittings and joints and minute surface details loomed large through this looking glass, and I remembered once again what it felt like to design and craft jewelry in the gold and silversmithing classes I took as electives at art school.

Furthermore, unlike cars or boats, this was not a moving object. It was an object to be used at rest; planted, stable, static. While it was to be portable, its forms hardly needed to be aerodynamic. This was another exercise in shifting design lenses; and in many ways, it was a more taxing adjustment than that required for a hundred-and-five-foot boat.

Our route, as always, was lit by questions and more questions. As so often happens when informed amateurs get involved, things tend to get turned around and tried upside down and backwards.

It was indeed the back view upon which we focused. We were now suddenly aware of the computerscape all around us, and what registered was that portion of its architecture most visible as we walked through the administration offices. It wasn't a pretty sight.

The computer we eventually designed had the fully integrated fluidity the client was looking for. As we were used to doing with cars, we treated it as an organically whole form, one whose rear and sides were considered of equal importance to its frontal working surface. Collaborating closely with the engineers, we had become knowledgeable about the size, location, and function of its critical inner workings and were able to formulate a highly flexible computing tool, one that could be used conventionally or with its easily detachable screen wall-mounted. And it was possible to fold this workstation into a compact package for transportability. The treatment of the backside with which we were so concerned featured a uniquely sculpted array of undulating cooling vanes and an integrated carrying handle. All surfaces and planes were interrelated and graced with precedent-breaking flowing forms that seemed to welcome human touch.

The up-close-and-personal detailing required for a project of this scale again enlarged our design palette. While the boat had stretched our visual reach, the RDI computer helped strengthen our small-design muscle capabilities, precisely those most needed to hyperfinesse and luxuriously detail the Infiniti J30, the car upon which we were simultaneously working.

RDI Computer

* * *

The YONtech 105 Yacht and RDI Computer were but two of a wildly diverse group of product design commissions NDI has accepted. Each one exposed the staff to the workings of alien industries, markets, technologies, and product environments. While some of this experience has led to immediate and specific application in unexpected ways, much of it has simply served to increase our range of exposure and broaden the possible perspectives we might bring to bear on any future task. Yet another portion of the experience appears at first entirely useless, inconsequential, even trivial. And it is here we look for the greatest inspiration, precisely because it is least expected.

Recall the impact that the daycare furniture project had on our understanding of the critical importance of *creative questions before creative answers*. Our involvement with the Angeles Group continues now with the development of a line of preschool tricycles. Far from the four-wheeled world of our everyday concerns, this is surely the product most evocative of childhood imagination. The tricycles we're currently playing with, both literally and figuratively, feature tubular frames flowing in playfully exaggerated sweeps. They are punctuated by miniature seats and other delicate details that would not be out of place in a surreal landscape by Salvador Dali or Paul Klee; they look as though they materialized right out of a child's dream.

While there are a host of legal, technological, and safety parameters to consider in designing a car, we discovered that golf clubs are perhaps an even more restrictive product. The PGA rule book covering what might and might not be done to a driver reads like a warden's guidelines for what might and might not be done during free time in the prison yard. The possible configurations of the shaft and club head are severely restricted, and even the pattern and depth of the texture inscribed on the hitting face is thoroughly prescribed. But by the careful selection and manipulation of color, finish, and graphics, as well as the fashioning of a subtle bulge beneath the grip of the club, NDI's work for Taylor Made resulted in the famed Bubble Burner. Probably our most successful single product, it shot past Big Bertha as the biggest-selling driver of all time. Yet, the range of our design work was far more circumscribed than that for any car. We remain deeply impressed by the potential impact of the most minuscule adjustments of color, graphics, and a little nudge of form.

Dealing with another culture's dust revealed some surprising insights I can't imagine we would have received in any other way. Toshiba approached NDI when it wanted to step outside the me-too styling of vacuum cleaners pervading the market in Japan. They were petite by Western standards, and we gasped with disbelief when we saw the lunch-bag sized receptacle for dirt collection.

"Surely," I said, "this would need changing too often."

"Yes," answered a Toshiba executive, "every few months can be quite an intrusive schedule."

How could that be possible, we all wondered, knowing that in our own homes such a bag would need changing every other day. To explain, a Toshiba engineer neatly demonstrated a profound cultural distinction. He placed two pieces of carpet side by side on the studio floor and invited the Americans present to trample all over one while the Japanese were to walk on the other. We would then vacuum each rug with different cleaners and examine the contents of the dirt receptacles. Just as we were to begin, we were asked to wait a moment, at which point the Japanese all leaned over simultaneously and did what Japanese always do at such moments: They removed their shoes. "Ah sooo!" we all proclaimed, thereby learning a dirty little cultural truth about ourselves.

Toshiba vacuum cleaner prototype, with integrated, unique bumper-handle

Rather than the somewhat imprecise, noisy, occasionally even crude character of many of the vacuum cleaners conceived for North American homes, our concept for Toshiba was atypically compact, precise, and tidy. The design reflected a surprising and utterly alien approach to the management of household dirt. We learned that even a task as common as vacuuming could not be assumed universally consistent, which had the effect of keeping us on our toes whenever we were confronted with an everyday activity whose very familiarity led us to believe we already knew everything we needed to know.

The rush received from exposure to new worlds can be highly energizing to the imagination. Nothing is more invigorating or elsewhere-taking to me than those wonderful title sequences and establishing shots at the opening of any good film, my favorite part of the movie-going experience. The immediate whiff of small-town Americana in *To Kill a Mockingbird, Something Wicked This Way Comes,* and *Hoosiers;* the open-sea, salty adventure promised at the opening of *Clear and Present Danger* and *Hunt for Red October;* the darkly claustrophobic menace of New York streetnights in the set-up shots of Sidney Lumet and Martin Scorsese; the icily remote yet psychologically up-close intensity at the outset of virtually all the films of Ingmar Bergman. We happily yield two or three hours of our valuable time following these sequences, compelled by the promise of experiencing the (sometimes improbable) life that might be lived out in these worlds.

Of course, the romance of small towns, big cities, remote isles, or naval destroyers is eventually lost on their actual occupants. It is often those of us called in from elsewhere, skilled amateurs and outsiders, who most readily grasp their significance and creative potential.

Engaging in work beyond the comfortable scope of everyday experience is not only a matter of exposure to different problems. It is the sense of entering wholly foreign and distinct universes and, drawing on our own resources, imagining what we might do in them. While designing yachts, we were mentally operating on the high seas of the Mediterranean. While envisioning children's furniture, we were operating on the classroom floor, back among the crayons and blocks.

Such excursions into unfamiliar turf also increase our appreciation for our home turf, in our case the very special rewards of designing cars. We have often debated which moment of gratification is the most delicious: the instant of conceptualization; the realization of the idea into three dimensions; the gelling of the group around the concept into a creative unit; the initial production model rolling off the assembly line; the first sighting of the car as it zips by on the street; the impact of seeing multiples of the design alter the visual landscape; or sliding behind the wheel and driving off into the sunset. Perhaps my own favorite is the sight of a child on the floor with a toy replica of the design, rolling it back and forth, imagining.

Nevertheless, any job over time can become routine, and we use any number of means to break the regularity. We take coffee breaks, talking breaks, lunch breaks. We take weekends, holidays, and vacations. We use sick days as mental health days, and some of us even take sabbaticals.

While there are times we simply crave shutting all the systems down, the more frequent need is to interrupt the daily rhythm and step back from a singular, myopic focus. Most people return from breaks rejuvenated and happy to have done more work, but other kinds of work—such as fixing or building something, cleaning out the garage, or merely rearranging the bookshelves. *Drinking from diverse wells*, however, introduces the notion of getting away from work *at work*.

The secret lies in the personal freedom to change the focus, pace, and direction of our labors from time to time. Just as we can extend aerobic activity by using different muscles, we can extend and enhance our powers of focus and creativity by shifting mental gears.

Encouraged to occasionally go off on tangents, and further enabled by the strategy of *blurring the boundaries*, the NDI staff is free to develop secondary regions of interest and development. While it is not a requirement, most people have seized this opportunity, and many now wear two or more hats at work. The results, not surprisingly, have benefited the company as well as the employee.

***

After hearing an unusually stimulating lecture in San Diego by Betty Edwards, the author of *Drawing on the Right Side of the Brain* and other books, I offered anyone at NDI who was interested the opportunity to take a week-long course with her. There have been quite a few takers over the years, but no one has been more affected by the experience than Jeff Fusco, a studio engineer.

Based on the Nobel prize–winning work of psychologist Roger Sperry, Edwards uses drawing techniques to nudge people out of sole reliance on linear, logical thinking by providing access routes to the joys of visual, nonlinear intuition. While doing his assigned homework one evening, Fusco became so lost in the exercise that he was startled when asked by his roommate if he was planning on going to bed anytime soon. "Why do you want to know?" Jeff asked, perplexed. Having begun working after dinner and assuming that only a few hours had passed, he could hardly believe it when he realized it was 3:00 A.M. So engaged was he in the zero-gravity, omnidirectional world of nonsequential thinking, he had lost all track of linear time. A new experience, it felt both unnerving and liberating.

By the end of the week, this highly organized and logical engineer, one who had "never before drawn a straight line without a straight edge," was sketching recognizable likenesses of Einstein. One of his delicate drawings appears in the latest edition of Edwards' book. More important, he had unlocked a whole new dimension of himself and blossomed in multiple directions simultaneously.

Away from work he became a serious painter, an activity he has pursued daily in the almost ten years since taking the course. Certainly, his new visualization skills helped him to both see his work more clearly and communicate it more effectively. He has also emerged as one of the champions of the use of leading-edge communications and computer graphics software at NDI, exploring new ways to visualize the designers' emerging concepts. In so doing, he has become unique among engineers—in reaching back toward design to find the creative means of closing a visualization gap that has traditionally been the sole concern of designers. He has also become NDI's filmmaker, recording presentations and making touching, documentary-style mementos for departing Japanese dispatches who work for a period of time at NDI. He has built a complete video department and well-equipped film library. All the while, he has grown as an engineer, in directions that would be inconceivable if his emerging interests had not been welcomed at work.

Like Mr. Fusco, Don Sondys, a modeler, has demonstrated interest and talent in performing as a designer from time to time. Both have contributed significantly to our nonautomotive projects. Sondys has dreamed up concepts for everything from computers to hi-fi speakers to graphic designs selected by the clients, often over competing solutions submitted by full-time designers. Rather than feeling threatened by this intrusion into their turf, however, the designers generally feel relieved at the extra help they're getting.

Vic Kazakevich, a modeler in the Interior Design Studio, had sculpted countless door trims, seats, and other soft automotive furniture. Recognizing the need to occasionally produce real cloth prototypes, he began to learn how to sew, and now has his own area of the studio where he shapes foam, sews, and produces seats and trims we can sit in and touch. Kazakevich has become NDI's (and probably one of the industry's) few seamster/modelers.

Matt Wilson, a modeler and fine painter, has found new ways of using the computer to develop three-dimensional surfaces. He now sculpts in clay and on the terminal with great proficiency. He goes back and forth between an analytic and tactile mode, forging new ways to communicate with designers, engineers, and even with the concept itself. He has not only *blurred the boundaries* between several disciplines, but along with Fusco and others, has established some entirely new wells from which we can all drink.

While many of these individuals have literally created new departments or spent time doing the work of adjoining disciplines, most have continued doing their original jobs. But they have been refreshed, expanded, and reoriented in the process. There are, of course, occasions when scheduling conflicts arise, and these must be resolved in concert with management. But the appeal of realizing these intrinsically motivated excursions into other kinds of work is so great that the staff is generally self-regulating in this regard.

These outward-spiraling interests continue, of course, beyond the confines of work. But wherever they are being pursued, the key is that the boundaries between home and office, life and work have blurred. I often run into significant numbers of people working and playing around with their various pursuits when I am around the office during lunchtimes, on weekends, or even over holidays. Wilson can often be found designing and building jazz guitars (he is an excellent jazz musician) on the computer and in the shops. Kazake-vich is continually making furniture fabrics, motorcycle seat covers, or adjusting sleeves or mending torn pants for friends. Fusco paints, not only with brush and canvas, but mouse and screen. And when some technique, image, or concept strikes any one of them as hav-ing unexpected application, they are just as likely to switch over to work on a current NDI project during these free-time excursions. The building has become a home away from home, a place from which it is not necessary to escape for refreshment. We have learned that, when a company lets life into work, the work it pro-duces becomes imbued with life.

***

Every company, of course, needs expertise, highly developed capabilities, and a deep understanding of its core business. Every *creative* company needs, in addition, continuing exposure to skill sets, technologies, orientations, and methodologies outside its area of expertise. Whether by attending conferences in unrelated profes-sions, practicing cross-disciplinary role-playing, or taking on atypi-cal business ventures, the goal is to avoid narrow specialization and a singular point of view.

This *drinking from diverse wells*, this intermixing of broad, general-ized experience with focused, honed skills, dramatically heightens the prospects for the kind of thinking that elicits "aha" or "now, why didn't we that of *that* before!" *Drinking from diverse wells* has maintained NDI's posture of skilled, open, and enthusiastic ama-teurs rather than narrow experts and tired pros.

And it has led to the realization that a little bit of knowledge about a lot of subjects is a dangerously creative thing.

PART IV

Synthesis

Uniting is a greater and more deserving art. An artist in uniting would be welcome in any profession, the world over.

Goethe[1]

To every thesis there is an antithesis and to this there is a synthesis. Truth is a never dying process.

Rollo May[2]

Experience in literal terms is a categorizing, a placing in a system of concepts. Metaphoric combination leaps beyond systematic placement, explores connections that were before unconnected.

Jerome Bruner[3]

10

Informed Intuition

The three vice presidents of design I served under at General Motors—Bill Mitchell, Irv Rybicki, and Chuck Jordan—were all utterly different from one another in style and temperament but shared a fervent commitment to the importance of creativity and to its protection in a hostile environment.

Unfortunately, they also implicitly agreed on how creativity should be protected. They assumed that when their "creative types" were weighed down with information about the obstacles, the market, the costs, the technological limits, or even the legal requirements of a product, they would tend "to design with nine-pound pencils," a characteristically colorful phrase of Mitchell's that was recited across generations with regularity and certainty.

Genuinely believing that they were safeguarding the creative process itself, they kept the design staff largely in ignorant bliss, free to dream up visions untethered by earthly realities. The studios at GM were decorated, as a result, with an unending display of sexy, exotic, lethal-looking designs that were impossible to build, would require doing a form of the Limbo dance to enter, and were largely irrelevant. Many referred to them as "styling wallpaper." I wondered what there was to be creative *about* in the absence of obstacles.

What these three powerful design leaders were acting on was the popular view of "creative types" as emotional dreamers, talented but undisciplined thinkers easily intimidated by the obstructions represented by real-world issues, playing with half-baked ideas without rigor, logic, or firm foundation. They were half-right.

While thinking innovatively does involve play, emotions, talent, and dreams, it also demands the fusion of these with clear-headed rationality, relentlessly hard work, and a firm, sober-eyed grasp of reality. For me, creative thought is, and always has been, the marriage of passion and logic, intuition and information, free imagination and the discipline of mastered skills. In reality, far from being blocked, it is positively fueled by hard information and stimulated by obstacles.

Yet, GM's curious view of creativity persists far beyond its corridors. It is a romantic notion that has been reinforced by countless biographies, novels, and films of naif-like, tortured geniuses: frail Chopin, mad Van Gogh, suicidal Schumann, raging Beethoven, extravagantly quirky Oscar Wilde. We have simultaneously eulogized and marginalized the most extreme examples of creative genius and assumed they represent the underlying nature of the process itself. What we have tended to discount are the far greater number of less juicy but more balanced life stories of the boringly normal, healthy geniuses: the businessman/composer Charles Ives, the happily well-adjusted Haydn and Dvořák, the stable and resourceful painters Rubens and Tiepolo, and the playfully brilliant, bongo-beating physicist Richard Feynman.

I am as much a fan of embattled, haunted geniuses and extremes of the human psyche as the next person, but creative activity has too often been marginalized as unmanageable, esoteric, and ungrounded.

It is not the sole domain of esoteric characters, nor is it an entertaining, exotic extra—the icing on the cake. Human creativity *is* the cake.

And it needs desperately to be loosened from some of its ancient, exaggerated, and dangerously false associations, which have tended to isolate the process from two of the fuels it most urgently requires: involvement and information. When properly connected to everyday issues and realities, creativity is arguably the most cogent and comprehensive mental means at our disposal of coping resourcefully with them.

Of course, this book is not about genius; nor is it confined to the needs of "creative types." It is about those factors in a work environment that foster idea-making—by anyone—as well as those that do not. And one of the most glaringly misunderstood and misused of the essential factors is the handling of information; how it is gathered, processed, and disseminated.

***

The seeds for what would ultimately lead to the development of a new department and perhaps even a new profession were planted during the earliest years of NDI's existence. It was during the first full-scale assignment, the redesign of Nissan's line of light trucks scheduled for release to the market in mid-1986, that we realized we had a problem accessing the kind of information needed to develop new concepts.

Nissan can justifiably claim that it initiated the highly profitable light truck market in North America when it introduced an awkward little pickup called the Datsun in 1953. The Datsun was so successful that its name became synonymous with that of the entire company. This led to the painful and costly necessity of reestablishing the original corporate name, Nissan, one which has never quite taken root in this country as firmly as Datsun did.

With virtually every major competitor having introduced its own version of these inexpensive utility vehicles by the early eighties, it was clearly time to reestablish the corporation's presence in the field. So we set about trying to understand just what a truck had come to mean to its users.

We began by becoming truck drivers, using our own and those of our competitors for the tasks for which they were evidently designed. And we read all the available literature and criticism. But we needed further input, and naturally reached out to the marketing group. What we received in response proved to be of somewhat limited use, even though their report read like a compendium of everything anyone would ever need to know about trucks.

To be fair, this project occurred during the early years of NDI and represented the first opportunity for many of the marketers to interact conceptually with a design group. Their only previous contact with design development had been in providing information on the character of the American market to the design group in Atsugi, Japan. Still, the information received was identical in form and substance to the kind of marketing input I'd seen earlier in Detroit.

The nature of the widespread rift between traditional sales-oriented marketing and design parallels exactly the one between most organizations and the creative process. It is widely assumed that marketing relies on analysis, design on synthesis; marketing people communicate with numbers and words, designers with pictures and forms; marketing aspires to an objective science, design to a subjective art; marketing professionals deduce from information and data, designers intuit from associations and experience. And both deal with the future, but from entirely distinct vantage points in the here and now.

In reality, the split between them is not nearly so clean—good marketers intuit and have ideas while designers analyze and grapple both with numbers and the hard sciences. There is clearly a need to *blur the boundaries* between these interdependent disciplines, neither of which can reach its ultimate effectiveness without the other.

But idea-making requires some additional ways of collecting and disseminating information. Too often, "objective" surveys, polls, and product clinics lead to sweeping generalizations about the kinds of people who can be counted on to behave in certain ways because they behave in certain *other* kinds of ways; and also, simply because they have done so before. So, for example, all those attracted to *this* kind of cereal/watch/television program/cell phone will surely want *that* kind of running shoe/movie-ending/senator—or car. I recall one cultural anthropologist/marketing "expert" (no longer in Nissan's employ) sharing his deep concern with the corporation as to NDI's suitability for designing a luxury car such as the Infiniti J30 since none of us wore Rolexes!

At the time of the truck project, personal contact between design and either sales or marketing was discouraged. Actually, it was disallowed. (Things have changed dramatically in this regard since that time.) Once again, the "creatives" were being protected by a well-intentioned but misguided policy, one with no grasp of the vital relationship between information and imagination. And so, we cheated.

We entered into a dark period of secret contacts, passed notes, and clandestine calls. From furtive eye-contacts, pithy comments, and knowing little half-smiles, it was relatively easy to identify those at marketing who didn't fully buy in, who saw their reports not as ends in themselves, but partial beginnings, and who sensed (but were not threatened by the fact) that the needs of conceptual thinking at the beginning of product development were distinct from those of sales at the other end of the process.

***

"Sheldon, can we talk?" I asked in unnecessarily hushed tones over the phone one morning.

"Sure, this is a good time," responded Sheldon Payne, product planning manager for marketing at the time. "What do you need to know?"

"I don't know," I replied, and we proceeded to engage in a series of meandering, wonderfully unfocused conversations about life and design and truckers and trucks. I wanted to hear about the information gathered for the report on the truck market *before* it had been collated, tidied up, and made presentable. And I wanted some of Mr. Payne's own professional but not necessarily scientific hunches and reactions to what he had learned. Even the small, seemingly innocuous observations seemed important to my gaining an intimate understanding of this market.

"It's kinda weird," he said. "Turns out that, even though truckers are very knowledgeable and demanding about such things as hauling load capacities and 'bed' dimensions and such, they almost never carry anything around in them."

"Really," I responded, growing intrigued.

"Yep. Seems they use their trucks *as trucks* less than twenty-five percent of the time," he continued.

"What do they use them as the rest of the time?" I wondered.

"Basic transportation. Cars."

There. A small, barely detectable synaptic spark. The truck trisected itself in my mind into three discrete boxes: one for carrying the engine, one the driver, and one the cargo. Seen in this formulation, it became dramatically evident that the former and latter were quite ample, but between them they sandwiched a rather stingy, cramped volume for the human cargo. And yet, according to Sheldon Payne's information, it was precisely this middle box that was most important and received the greatest use.

We proceeded to shift our design priorities for the truck. We enlarged the cabin, lengthened the doors for ease of entrance and egress, raised the roof, and increased visibility in all directions.

While not sacrificing the dimensions of the truck bed, the Nissan Hardbody, as it came to be known, stood out among its competition at the time with a subtly altered proportion, one that spoke clearly to the real-world uses of the vehicle.

Our direction for this project came from a neutral, even passive perusal of the marketing input. It was not a matter of manipulating the data or forcing it to comply with any preconceived notions. Too often, marketing uses its data (or the corporation uses marketing) to control the outcome of its findings in order to fit a preordained direction. The issue is one of control, as well as the avoidance of having to deal with the discomfort and threat of the unexpected or the novel. While a sense of control might be maintained, however, some strikingly useful (and profitable) new ideas are rendered invisible.

***

When times are tough and risk-avoidance is in the air, nothing can provide a greater illusion of security than statistics. But the greatest danger is when these are used not to inform the concept or decision-making process, but to replace it.

Answers cannot be found at the bottom of a column of digits. "Statistics," said W. C. Fields, "are like a bikini. What they reveal is suggestive, what they hide, vital." Fields was a funny and dirty old man, but his comment reveals a simple truth that seems to be lost on the majority of political and corporate leaders today. Even when there are no corporate politics in play, the very attempt to simplify and clarify the complexities, discontinuities, and contradictions of life outside corporate walls distorts what is being observed.

This might be acceptable to those who were satisfied with executive summaries—"Skip the stuff in the middle and cut to the bottom line"—but not to the folks groping for the potential lurking in the complexities of the present moment—"Skip the bottom line and just give us the stuff in the middle!"

What we required was a fresh approach to touching the users of our products and deploying what we learned. The traditional mode, with its penchant for bottom-line clarity, order, and conclusiveness, was far too blunt a tool for our needs. We were not looking for answers, we were looking to witness all the complex, ambiguous, and contradictory evidence of real-world activities and issues to build a springboard and a context for our concepts.

We had seen how much we had learned from our interaction with Mr. Payne, with whom we freely deconstructed, then reconstructed, the previously collected marketing information. Now we began to wonder just how much had been lost or tainted by the collection process itself. Surely, there were ways of accessing input in addition to written questionnaires and quantified surveys. And we desperately wanted to defocus the focus groups and product clinics.

However, at this point, we knew a great deal more about what we did *not* want than what we did. We intuited that something valuable was being distorted and perhaps even lost in the incessant need to analyze and quantify what was essentially a qualitative, subjective experience. In his important book, *Trust in Numbers: The Pursuit of Objectivity in Science and Public Life*, science historian Theodore M. Porter points out that there is "often a willingness to leave untouched the most important issues in order to deal objectively with those that can be adequately quantified."[1]

Given the bias of our educational systems and work environments, most people draw a blank trying to imagine a responsible alternative to segmented, analytic thought. Clearly, collecting more numerical confetti was not the answer.

Furthermore, there was something very wrong about the corporate attitude toward the future and what to do about it. The unstated and absurd assumption was that it already existed somewhere as an inevitability, and our task was to second-guess it. This was to be accomplished by asking lots of people lots of questions about how they might like something *to be*, whether a movie-ending, cereal taste, front-end design, or political strategy. The catch, however, was the "to be" part. The topspin given to the questions on surveys suggested that the answers were somehow representative of future reactions rather than what they really were: current responses in a present (and highly artificial) context.

Designers and anyone else in the corporation dealing with that which is not yet in existence have traditionally been thought of as futurists. And many designers have accepted this romantic and utterly unsupportable notion. But at NDI we have never dwelled on the future for original thoughts. Rather, we dwell on sensing, studying, experiencing, and ingesting *the present*. Any thought we might have about the future is a "presenthought." There is no such thing as a "futurethought." But, since many people use language and concepts from the past to deal with the confusion of the present (think: "politicians"), anyone who deals imaginatively with the potential latent in the current moment is perceived as a futurist. In fact, NDI is filled with committed "now-ists."

Which means that designers are not in the business of second-guessing the future after all, but of shaping it. And this is not a mind-set that rests easily with current corporate assumptions or professional "futurists."

George Bernard Shaw said, "If I bind the future I bind my will. If I bind my will I strangle creation."[2] It is certainly not surprising that traditional data-based social research is not beloved by those in the corporation who are busy doing what they believe businesses really do—which is to give form to the future based on an imaginative grasp of the potential latent in the current moment. The alternative is the *equally risky* reiteration of a well-researched past—the future as "The Present, Part II."

What *was* surprising was when the parent company asked NDI to establish its own marketing department.

***

The Japanese have a wonderfully insatiable curiosity about other cultures, and the design-view, they felt, was yet another way of accessing it. They wanted to understand the world in which our sometimes strange (to their eyes) forms and concepts made sense. This was clearly an opportunity to extend the impact of design within the organization, but we were loathe to now practice what we had preached against. However, Nissan had been impressed with the view we had provided of the North American market through our designs and wanted to add these to the findings of the marketing group in Los Angeles, its own researchers, as well as outside consultancies such as the Yankelovich Monitor.

As with each of the other strategies we evolved at NDI, this new activity was defined by the needs of the *creative priority*. Rather than categorizing and segmenting the market for the assumed needs of sales, we began a long journey to find ways of more fully understanding the culture in which we lived to build a context from which our ideas would grow and within which they would make sense. And we believed that planning and sales, too, would find much of value from the broader, more all-encompassing perspectives of the creative set.

It has not been an easy journey. At the time we began the process, there was virtually nowhere to look for reference or guidance, although by what seemed at the time sheer chance, I found a soulmate and source of encouragement at Stanford University. While serving on a National Endowment for the Arts architecture and design panel in Washington, D.C., I had occasion to read through several long applications for grants from graduate business and engineering schools. Institutions such as Carnegie Mellon, MIT, Stanford, Berkeley, and others had drafted proposals incorporating design into their programs in one form or another, and all had some merit. But one day I came across a rather esoteric and nearly unfathomable paper which had been passed over by the panel, and it stayed on my mind. I reread it that evening, came back to the next day's meeting, and said, "I'm not a hundred percent certain what the hell this is about, but I'd love to find out." As a result, something called the Process for Change Lab at Stanford's graduate business school happily received a substantial grant.

About six months later, after an address I gave at the school of architecture at Stanford, a petite but mighty package of energy approached me at the podium and matter-of-factly announced, "Some day, we're going to do some things together, you and I." Although I had not yet heard her name, it didn't take long for me to realize that this woman was the author of the grant I had championed in Washington.

Although Sara Little Turnbull and I were from vastly different backgrounds, we had both been imagining some radically new means of tracking, ingesting, and creatively using information about the culture in which we lived and worked. A vast, astute, and insatiable reader, she had, over a period of decades, compiled a massive library of articles, artifacts, pictures, and clippings. These she assembled according to categories that cut across more traditional boundaries, like color (by country), attitudes towards health, aging, fitness, and the like. This file-on-everything is arrayed in tidy cabinets that fill her rooms at the graduate business school. They were purchased by Stanford as the core of her Process for Change Lab, and are made available on a contractual basis to companies like Ford, Nike, or Nissan, along with her wizardry at mining them for unexpected themes, good questions, unlikely connections, and other assorted nuggets.

NDI eventually moved in its own unique direction, somewhat less global and more dependent on the development of personal relationships and direct experience than readings. But it was enormously helpful at the time to have a link with someone who thoroughly understood what we were trying to do. And perhaps most important, what I wanted to develop at NDI was exactly the kinds of tracking-antennae and sensitivities that alerted both Sara and me, amid all the "noise" of our daily lives, to each other in the first place.

✳✳✳

Shortly after learning of Nissan's request, we hired Sheldon Payne away from the marketing group to manage this new department as well as to help create a color and fabric studio, which the parent company had simultaneously requested. Along with a background that included experience in engineering and planning, he also had a deep understanding and an unusually sensitive eye for color. A studio was born comprising color on the one hand and our new effort to monitor the market on the other.

The connections between these two areas are not nearly as remote as they might at first appear. With virtually no functional determinants to guide it, future directions for color are heavily dependent on alert and imaginative "readings" of the cultural climate. The ability to sense the potentially global resonance of a hue such as eco-green in the early nineties, the appropriateness of bronze and eggplant to a golf club, or pale violet and grayed-down green to preschool furniture, relies on a keen awareness of social priorities and the mood of the times.

This new complex was called the White Studio, white being the presence of all colors. And since we were dedicated to informing the designers' intuitions with a greater understanding of the context within which they worked, we called our new not-marketing department the Design Context Laboratory (DCL).

Staffing such an enterprise presented an enormous challenge, as there were no established university programs that provided context researchers. We cast our nets wide, finding potential candidates among writers, cultural anthropologists, and various social scientists, but not in the ranks of classically educated market researchers, whom we found hopelessly well indoctrinated. Even Sheldon Payne said it took him more than a year "to go through decompression" from his prior environment and orientation.

Everyone to whom we were attracted seemed to have exceptionally wide-ranging interests and multiple majors in school. Nick Backlund was the quintessential choice, and quickly became the DCL supervisor. He had majored in both English literature and philosophy, but upon spending his junior year in Paris, switched his major to art history. (His father was a founding editor of the *Smithsonian* magazine.) Before joining NDI, Backlund had been a bartender in a Parisian café, a film actor, a newspaper reporter, a writer, and an associate editor for *International Design* magazine in New York, where we finally found him.

Peter Coughlan, whom Nick later discovered, was no less broadly educated. After receiving his B.A. in English literature, he taught English as a second language to Saudis, Swiss, French, and Spanish peoples in England and Portugal, which proved to be wonderful experience for helping people really see the character and idiosyncracies of their *own* cultures and languages. He then went on to study anthropology and psychology, but received his Ph.D. in applied linguistics. His doctoral dissertation committee, however, were all psychologists and anthropologists.

What Messrs. Payne, Backlund, and Coughlan all share in abundance is a zest for full immersion in what is happening around them. With the multitude of perspective points they bring to bear, even the most commonplace of events and interactions seem filled with riches for creative consideration. Everything is simultaneously reflected in minute detail and from widely separated vantage points. Don Gifford, in his excellent book *The Farther Shore: A Nat-*

ural History of Perception, said that "perception takes its shape from the physical givens of the world while creatively shaping the physical world in turn." And he added that "the capacity of perception to shape and reshape is both influenced by and gives rise to those more formal historical presences we call ideas."[3]

Yet, our three design researchers have no seeming need to impose any personal agenda or added significance to what they report. They are the antithesis of spin doctors, being content, even committed, to deliver information knuckleballs to the extent that is humanly possible. And it is precisely this neutrality, this lack of need for manipulating their observations, which affords them such an abundance of access to facets of experience either hidden or distorted by biased reporting.

Nor is there any evident need to stereotype, simplify, or impart an underlying essence to explain what they perceive. Operating as much like social artists as social scientists, what they talk about with us is not a distilled, tidied-up version of reality, but rather the infinitely layered, messy, and often maddeningly self-contradictory nature of real life.

***

When beginning our work on the second-generation Quest minivan, we once again perused the marketing reports made available to us. These were now vastly more useful to the design staff, who had even been invited to participate in their formulation by a marketing group ever more open to our input.

Evolving one of our own designs always presents certain challenges, especially when the first generation has been deemed a success. We needed to distance ourselves from the product as though some other group had created it, in order to start from a relatively clean, unbiased position. Yet, we did not want to damage what had already been well received and appreciated.

Surprisingly, some of the marketers suggested we lengthen the vehicle three inches. They explained that, while the overall dimensions of the Quest were appropriate, there simply wasn't adequate room behind the rear seats for carrying additional cargo. The three-inch figure, while not of great consequence, nagged at us. How, we wondered, had the marketing group arrived at that specific and seemingly arbitrary figure?

The DCL had initiated its own researches at the same time. Rather than working independently and reporting to the company, Backlund's group acted like scout leaders to the designers, guiding them on anthropological excursions, including them on the observational team. In the quest for creative thinking, research should never be left to someone else, as nothing so stimulates the imagination as the impact of direct experience.

In the case of the minivan, scores of owners were invited to come to NDI *with their vehicles*, which they were asked to bring in whatever state of tidiness or disarray they were in. We spoke with them openly, directly. No one-way mirrors or hidden cameras. No facilitators or intermediaries unfamiliar with the product being considered. No lengthy questionnaires or surveys.

Instead, there was much animated talk about how each interacted with their vehicles, what worked well, what didn't. And we went for rides with them, anything to tease out hidden problem areas or opportunities. As much or more was learned from simple observation of their unselfconscious actions, all the minute rituals performed before even starting the engine. We noted the ways they made themselves comfortable; where they tossed their "carry-on items," whether on the floor, the seat next to them, or behind them; how some readjusted mirrors and seats each time upon reentry; the fascinating collections of items stored in various compartments and pockets we had provided, and the even more fascinating opportunities for storage *they* had found. Much of this valuable input would not have been thought worth mentioning by the participants, let alone asked about on the marketing questionnaires.

As important as the information was, the persons for whom we were designing had suddenly become real to us. We continued to think about and refer to these individuals by name or memorable action throughout the project. This was a far cry from the depersonalizing impact of reading about "the market" or "boomers," or "Xers" in formal reports.

Yet, there were no grand expectations. No one's performance was being judged by whether or not anything of value came from each encounter. It was, in this sense, true research; neutral, unbiased, inquisitive. And its real value would be ascertained later, from the perspective of any fresh departures or improvements to the product that resulted. This was in sharp contrast to the more traditional marketing methods of many companies, where the pressure is high for immediately demonstrable results, where the event is an end unto itself.

Upon completing our researches (which felt more like simple searches), we compiled our varied riches, mounting snapshots, scribbling memorable quotes, sketching the ingenious ways people had solved problems, creating large observational collages on the studio walls. We had not yet found any solutions or answers. Once again, our principal thrust had been to first find new and more pertinent questions.

As we stood back from this kaleidoscopic array of direct experience, however, one consistent theme did emerge. Virtually every participant in each of the groups said they wanted around six inches more room behind the third row of seats for extra cargo. And yet, simultaneously, the very same individuals unanimously praised the vehicle's maneuverability, the ease with which it could be parked. It was, they said, "just-right-sized," and pleaded with us to make it not one inch longer.

Confronted directly with these apparently contradictory requests, the designers set to work resolving the issue, *not the input*, which continued to haunt them for weeks. And, as with so many other mutual exclusivities, this one led to a mini-breakthrough. Bruce Campbell, the interior design chief on the project, suddenly flashed on a simple, vertical rack of shelves behind the third row of seats. With an exquisitely uncomplicated plastic bracket system attached to the side walls, one or two shelves could be moved up or down to accommodate considerably more than six inches of added cargo capacity *without increasing the vehicle's length*.

Groceries, for example, might now be arrayed in such a manner that the bags on the bottom would not be deformed by those on top. In the same horizontal space, two or three times the carrying capacity had been achieved by conceiving of the increase in volume along a *vertical* plane. As a further finesse, making the topmost shelf position the same height as the seatback provided a visual shield for anything of value, such as cameras, briefcases, or purses stored beneath it. For the first time in a minivan, there would be a secure, out-of-sight location for precious items, a solution to a further problem we had not initially set out to solve. The physicist Werner Heisenberg said, ". . . one can never overcome an isolated difficulty, but must always surmount several at once."[4]

This feature will be introduced on the forthcoming Quest minivan, scheduled to reach the dealers in North America later this year (1998). It will have resolved the apparently impossible request of making the vehicle bigger *without making it bigger*, by thinking in a different dimension from that of the original request.

And our solution helped to explain the confusing instruction from marketing to make the car three inches longer. They had clearly received the same information concerning the desire for more space without added length, but proceeded to eliminate the contradictory nature of their observations before disseminating them to the designers. By confining their thinking to a single plane, they saw fit to use an overly simple formula: Add six inches of desired increased storage space to zero inches of additional length, divide by two—and recommend three inches of compromise!

The information had once again been reduced to a quantified bottom line. While the designers would have been spared the challenge of dealing with what seemed like self-cancelling requests from the market, the product would have lost out on an innovation that synthesized the polarized positions and offered a unique and useful new feature. Information fed intuition resulting in innovation.

***

Inconclusive data. Contradictory input. Incomplete information. Overlapping matrices of thought. Disorder. Ambiguity. These are the realities we face when dealing with such vital issues as choice of mates, lifelong career paths, whether or not to have children, which house to buy, where to go on vacation, and all the other really important decisions in life. And most of us make good decisions for ourselves most of the time. So good, it is worth considering just how we do it. The best guideline for decision-making at work may well be the decision-making process we use at home, where it really counts.

Unusual as this suggestion might at first sound, it is surely more plausible than the reverse. It is hard to imagine spouses actually presenting fat reports filled with graphs and quantified preferences to each other or mining the results of objective surveys on whether they should buy a pet or take a trip. (Take the trip!)

What we realize at home with no difficulty whatsoever is that deductive logic simply runs out of gas (data) when used as the sole or even the primary mechanism for making such decisions. What we must also accept is the full deployment of our intuition at such times. We know, instinctively, that intuition positively thrives in such complex, chaotic, uncertain situations and leads us to "hold it all together" in a multifaceted, many-layered mental whole.

By synthesizing rather than analyzing, we do not become illogical or irrational; rather, we relax conscious control and engage our vast sorting and scanning powers, consider images, connections, and surprising metaphors that simply do not arise under logical, sequential, critical scrutiny. Using a far greater percentage of our mental capacities simultaneously, we find ourselves comfortable with all-important periods of ambivalence, a critical key to intuitive, creative thought.

It is out of such active ambivalence that imagery forms, leading us in directions that "feel right," seem like "elegant solutions," or have "the ring of truth." Such poetic terminology is enunciated not only by designers and artists, but by Nobel prize–winning mathematicians and physicists when explaining how they finally achieved their critical breakthroughs. The great French mathematician Henri Poincaré has written, "It may be surprising to see emotional sensibility involved a propos of mathematical demonstration which, it would seem, can interest only the intellect. This would be to forget the feeling of mathematical beauty, of the harmony of numbers and forms, of geometric elegance. This is a true aesthetic feeling that all real mathematicians know, and surely it belongs to emotional sensibility."[5] S. Chandrasekhar, the Nobel prize–winning astrophysicist, said, "It is, indeed, an incredible fact that what the human mind, at its deepest and most profound, perceives as beautiful finds its realization in external nature." And he further wonders, "How does it happen that beauty in the exact sciences becomes recognizable even before it is understood in detail and before it can be rationally demonstrated? In what does this power of illumination consist?"[6]

Well-developed intuitive skills require well-deployed antennae, considerable experience, and as much practice at *intelligently feeling* the tone and potential of a complex whole as skilled logical analysis and the use of the scientific method. And intuition demands the open sharing of undoctored information and considerable encouragement from executives long associated with cool, objective thinking.

"Spare me your hunches," barked Superintendent Jane Tennison to her detectives on the terrific British television police series "Prime Suspect." "Just the facts, m'aam," demanded Sergeant Joe Friday in "Dragnet." These are the admonitions we commonly receive in the workplace, where tough thinking is required. But not at home, where we're asked, "What do you *really* feel?" What we do for ourselves, we do best.

The creative process hungers for direct access to real-world issues and concerns. Far from being a romantic escape *from* disciplined thinking, genuine creative thought is an imaginative escape *with* disciplined thinking. Without a savvy command of the underlying principles of structural physics, Frank Lloyd Wright could never have realized the cantilevered thrill of "Fallingwater." Without Beethoven's consummate grasp of the mathematics of musical theory and notation, his symphonies would have remained silent cries of joy locked in his heart. Nor could the pristine beauty of Leonardo Da Vinci's science or the scientific underpinning of his art have emerged, one without the other.

Creativity is the mastery of information and skills in the service of dreams.

11

Porous Planning

We should have been thrilled. Nissan had once again concurred with our selected design direction from among the three alternatives we had brought to Japan in the form of one-fourth-scale clay models for consideration. The project was the design of the 1987 Pulsar NX (whose creation is discussed in Chapter 6). It had served as a fine example of how individuals can interact to spark unexpected, even unintended, reactions in one another. But this same project also caused great stress to the system, as the timing of the breakthrough that elevated the design from the ordinary to the extraordinary was wholly unexpected and unwelcomed by us and the Japanese.

Once we orient ourselves to the social and technological parameters of a product, grasp its price range and overall package dimensions, and reach general agreement on an appropriate definition, each designer goes off to independently explore his/her own directions for the first several months. While each works alone at this stage, there are nonetheless regular reviews and critiques where individual progress is shared with the group. Creative interaction is always encouraged, but so is a wide diversity of exploratory paths. Walking through the studios at this stage is like visiting a model-car toy store.

As we approached the scheduled model selection benchmark (about one-third of the way through the Pulsar NX project), it was first necessary to select the three concepts we felt had the most potential from the dozen or so being considered in Japan. But as we surveyed the results of our early labors, no one spotted any one toy they really wanted to play with or take home.

When working on a car that, like the Pulsar, is destined for the East as well as the West, the planners and executives of the parent corporation like to review and reach consensus on which of the concepts it should commit to for final development, a determination representing hundreds of millions of design, engineering, and development dollars. They inevitably ask which our preferred choice is, and why. Happily, in the seventeen years of our relationship, the corporation has agreed with our recommended directions virtually every time, a striking exception being the current line of Pathfinders.

While it is understandable for Nissan to expect a progress review a third of the way through a project, the problem is that idea-making does not necessarily progress progressively. It is rarely a sequential, tidy, consistently forward-moving process, and the point of departure that would eventually lead to the final design direction for this product had simply not yet occurred. So while we were comforted by their vote of support for the NDI-proposed design, our hearts were not yet fully in it. What had been chosen was eminently reasonable, but we were aiming for something considerably more compelling to energize us for the enormous task of resolving and fine-tuning the mountain of complex detail and interlocking parts composing the modern automobile.

Upon returning from our presentation in Japan, we reconvened to consider once again who and what this car was *for*. We reread the plan and the product definition, and arrived at the same place: This was a product to be used by anybody for just about anything. If its purpose were to be reduced to a single descriptor, it would be *diversity*. Diverse uses by diverse users. Great, we felt. We're lost and have no map.

The very ambiguity of our position stayed with us, conjuring only vague, shifting images. Rather than commencing the final refinement stage, everyone continued searching and circling around the accepted direction, looking for some relationship, gesture, or connection that might snap all the pieces together, something that would breathe life into the design. It was during this period that I inadvertently spotted one of Doug Wilson's doodles as I anxiously shuffled through the sketches on the designers' desks during one lunchtime break. Instantly, I saw in what he had drawn the potential for a modular car.

We now envisioned an automobile with several major panels that might be removed and replaced by other panels, allowing the owner to transform it from a coupe to a minivan to a small truck to a convertible. The Pulsar NX would become a mercurial, permutable little car, one that could shape-shift for a variety of functions, *all at the owner's whim*.

The essential factor leading to this discovery had lain embedded in our earliest researches and mindmaps and in the plan itself. We just had not been able to see it. The indistinct adjectives became ends in themselves rather than uncertain compass settings pointing everywhere at once and nowhere in particular. Ambiguity led to diversity led to modularity, which instantly became the organizing principle that caused the entire design to focus and gel into a coherent whole.

Pulsar NX concept and development sketches by author and Doug Wilson

This new way of seeing the product did not represent the kind of small-scale, evolutionary refinement that generally occurred after the formal approval of a design direction by key corporate planners and executives. Our excitement about the possibilities of a modular car and our confidence in its rightness for this particular product, however, carried us through any hesitations we might have felt about introducing such a bold departure so late in the process.

A multidisciplinary team was swiftly mobilized at NDI, and the entire vehicle transmogrified into something far more dynamic, expressive, and purposeful than what had been shown in Japan. Once again, the designers began following the design, which seemed now to possess a very certain sense of its own identity. We were on a fast track, and the immediate challenge was to get the rest of the corporation on the same one. We became fax, phone, and letter-writing machines, launching a vigorous but extremely late campaign for a considerable adjustment in our bearings.

Given the preoccupation of Nissan's engineers and planners with rigorous, authoritative planning, we fully expected some stiff opposition. We were working, however, with an atypical and uncommonly open-minded planning manager, Keiichi Shinohara, a purposeful man with an easy smile and a ready capacity for delight, who was a planner with an engineering background and a real passion for the product. We were to link up once again on the equally challenging Infiniti J30 project. Sensing our confidence and commitment, he quickly grasped the pertinence and significance of the breakthrough and, rather than seeing the change as destructive, understood how it actually strengthened the plan.

Shinohara-san was fully aware of his primary responsibility for the quality, reliability, build requirements, and cost targets of the product. Corporations seldom give extra points for innovation beyond the expected, but, of course, true innovation always exceeds the expected. Knowing the sheer quantity of engineering development that would be required, the product liability and certification issues involved, and the potential cost implications, Shinohara did not hesitate to pull the emergency cord on the product development train and abruptly switch tracks. With adrenaline, inspiration, and a sense of urgency now running high on both sides of the Pacific, a Herculean effort was mounted and the project was completed with no schedule delays.

When it was finally released, the first such mass-produced vehicle attracted worldwide attention and helped garner Nissan its first-ever Car of the Year award in Japan, an achievement with significant impact on both sales and prestige in that country. In America it became a steady best-seller in its category for years to come.

The three formulations of the Pulsar

I would like to be able to say that this response to an unexpected idea at an unanticipated time is typical of my experience with corporations. Unfortunately, it is not. Barriers abound in bureaucracies, and one of the most formidable is the strategic plan that stands above all for mature, responsible, and rational corporate procedure.

A plan of action is, of course, as vital to a program as an itinerary is to a trip, a sketch is to a painting, and an outline or synopsis is to a book. At its best, it maps out a region ripe for development and provides an overall focus and goal. No one is surprised when trips, paintings, and books stray from their prescribed paths; itineraries, sketches, and outlines are wisely designed with wide degrees of latitude.

Unfortunately, a strategic plan is seldom referred to as having been designed. Rather, it is often said to be *structured* or *erected*. It gathers supporters, loyalists who protect its integrity. Curiously, it is often classified by deeper levels of security and official secrecy than the end products to which it refers. Rather than continue to provide a map to a possible future, the plan too often becomes a static entity, rigid, resistant to change, an end in itself.

When new ideas erupt from the nonstatic world beyond the corporation, most will sacrifice the ideas for the sanctity of the plan, since it is considered weak if it has to change. Some corporations even define their plans to help distinguish between that which is in bounds and that which is out of bounds. For these companies, the world is divided into the realm of acceptable (predicted) ideas and unacceptable (unpredicted) ones, robbing the company of any possibility of fresh, leading-edge thinking. We have seen time and again how the strongest ideas are formed by the incorporation of something from a remote and utterly unconnected region. The line is thin and blurred between out-of-bounds thinking, which has been outlawed by the plan, and "out-of-the-box" thinking, which every executive boldly proclaims he/she wants and even demands.

If it is to thrive, imaginative thinking cannot be constrained by preconceptions or prior intentions, no matter how thoroughly researched, staunchly supported, and cogently presented. Creativity, it has been said, does not play *by* the rules, it plays *with* the rules.

Most corporate executives and managers are appalled at being surprised once a project is under way. Yet, the Harvard psychologist Jerome Bruner sets a minimum working definition of creativity precisely as "an act that produces *effective surprise*—this I take as the hallmark of the creative enterprise."[1] Being surprised means being (or appearing) unprepared, and this provokes the fear of a loss of respect and authority. Surprise, like change, is one of the great inducers of stress, even for those guilty of creating it. When something unanticipated appears, there is an immediate sense of loss of control over unseen forces that might encroach, invade, or otherwise alter the best-laid plans.

Herein lies the essential rub. Plan-making is one activity that can unintentionally curtail and even destroy creative thought and action in an organization. Even when confronting the very ideas it might need to fully succeed, there is a deeply ingrained reflex to reject an unexpected, unplanned-for concept, since it falls inconveniently outside the original plan.

✳✳✳

Looking back to evaluate what went *right* with a plan is an elusive task, as you can never be sure what might have happened on the road not taken. Still, it is worthwhile to ponder what can be learned from the parts of the strategy that worked, those that did not, and those that might have worked better—and why.

Due to some considerable flexibility and agility on the part of the planners, designers, and engineers at Nissan, the Pulsar NX was deemed an exceptionally distinctive, progressive product. While it sold well and turned an excellent profit, we can now see that it did not establish a permanent niche for the modular principle in the marketplace. Nissan ultimately elected not to develop this concept any further, so modularity passed from the scene with the last Pulsar manufactured in 1993.

From a midrange business perspective, the car was an undeniable success, but I have often wondered what else could have been done to establish an entirely new category of vehicle.

There were some serious aspects of the modular concept that remained unresolved even as the NX was first released for sale. While people reported that they were enjoying and utilizing its modularity, they had trouble finding a place to store the large and relatively cumbersome hatchback "upper" in the typically limited space of most garages. NDI conceived of some last-minute hook and pulley contraptions for garage mounting, but neither sales nor the dealers were eager to get into the hook and pulley business. And the Sportbak module that transformed the car most dramatically into a minivan was larger still. Dealers had real problems finding ample space for stocking the bulky cartons containing the modules.

It would be very easy to blame the lack of long-range success for the modular aspect of the car on the conservatism and stubborn resistance of sales, marketing, and the dealers. And we did at the time. But the fact is, we had not finished the job. Too often, those who introduce genuinely novel directions stop short of completing their tasks, handing the concepts off to the implementers and neglecting to deal with all the equally novel problems inevitably left in their wake.

Even if we had tried to finish the work, however, we could not have done so ourselves, as many of the new problems spawned by our concept fell into domains beyond our own. An organizational mechanism was needed to bring together all the necessary departments and disciplines to deal with the problems as they arose. This idea goes well beyond the notion of multidisciplinary "platform teams," since no one can anticipate at the outset of a project which areas of expertise might be required for dealing with a genuinely new departure. In this particular case we needed the further involvement of sales, marketing, public relations, and advertising, as well as engineering, design, and planning. Their input was essential *during the development stages* of the modular concept, not only in resolving issues that went beyond the expertise of the original team, but in identifying unanticipated deficiencies as well as further potential applications of the idea.

Just as many people tend to wait for the second generation of a newly introduced model until they "work out all the bugs," those departments not directly involved with the initial creation of an unscheduled new concept are dubious about embracing it right away. A real effort is required to overcome this skepticism as well as the to-be-expected resistance to the discomfort of the new.

Surprisingly, the ideal department for mobilizing such an effort turns out to be planning itself, not a discipline traditionally associated with spontaneity or change. Of course, this suggests a very different kind of activity and outlook than currently exists in most corporations. But it is one urgently required for those genuinely prioritizing the value of ideas. Ideally, planning should utilize its unique overview to provide an ongoing, synthesizing force for the duration of an undertaking. Its walls would become penetrable screens through which cutting-edge surprises and cross-disciplinary input might pass, from the inside out as well as the outside in.

***

For Nissan, by the early nineties, the famed 300ZX had virtually become "the franchise." It had won all the top design and engineering awards and prestigious races. The subject of a worldwide network of clubs and organizations, it had been used as the vehicle of choice in countless Hollywood films, and generated more free ink in the enthusiast press than all the company's other products combined. So well established was it in the automotive firmament that it did not even need to be identified with its full name; it had simply become the "Z." With a thoroughbred lineage dating back to the original, explosively successful 240Z, the 300ZX was the envy of its competitors, many of whom regarded it as one of the finest mass-produced performance machines ever.

High-performance sports cars had been such a staple in the industry from the very beginning that no one ever seriously questioned their role in the product lineup. They had achieved ever-higher levels of sophistication, luxury, speed, and handling, as well as insurance rates and prices. There seemed to be no limit to what people would pay for the sensual driving experience they promised. And for most automobile companies, they were inevitably the preferred vehicle category for introducing and demonstrating their technological prowess, creativity, and machismo. The sports car was the ultimate "halo product," believed to raise the reputation of the entire line by mere association.

Whenever it was time to introduce a new generation of such a car, no one felt the need to question its role or redefine it for a changing world. As a target, both the product and its market were considered givens, virtually immutable.

So no one noticed when the car gradually began to steer off-course during the late eighties. Its very success as an icon for that decade's preoccupation with excess and status proved to be its ultimate undoing in the nineties.

The market for such sexy cars as the Mazda RX7, the Corvette, the Porsche 911, as well as the "Z," dwindled to a fraction of its former strength in the nineties. An aging population found them increasingly uncomfortable and, given their limited practicality, harder and harder to justify. The more sober, less secure tenor of the time suddenly made usefulness appealing, and the high-priced luxury sports cars of the eighties were replaced by the now sexy and practical trucks, Jeeps, and sport utility vehicles. Among all the futurists, analysts, commentators, and experts attached to the automotive industry, not one had predicted the demise of the sports car.

Nor, for that matter, had any of the planners, with the sole exception of a small group at Mazda's California studios who championed a return to a far simpler, less costly direction in its Miata. The question is, how did an entire industry fail to read the change and plan for it?

At NDI, we have found that planning is most difficult when a product and its market have a long, well-established, and successful relationship. The planners' approach in the face of such sustained success is inevitably "to keep things going" and to "avoid fixin' it if it ain't leaking." Everyone has had time to become an expert, and there is no pressing motivation to wipe the slate clean and go through the unsettling, arduous business of starting from scratch. But it is precisely at such times that we have disciplined ourselves to start over as beginners, challenging traditional wisdom and checking for leaks in the assumptions.

As I write this, NDI is reconsidering the most stable staple of all, the basic four-door family sedan. We do not yet have the answer (and I couldn't share it with you if we did), but there is the sense in the studios that its meaning is about to shift. Interestingly, this seems to be happening at the very time when every other vehicle category is proudly proclaiming it has the smooth, quiet comfort and practicality of the sedan. So we have car-like sport-utes, car-like minivans, and even car-like trucks. The "car-car" (as NDI calls it) will either become redundant, grow into something new, or become extinct.

Of course, we may also discover that the existing assumptions are just fine. Even so, the act of reexamining them tends to lead to fresh, vital variations on an old theme. It is a question of going through the process of resetting our sights, as well as the location and viability of the target.

I have heard it said that planning is the "ready, aim" part of "ready, aim, fire!" This is at the heart of the conventional way of thinking about planning, and it is fine as far as it goes.

But there are some severe limits implied by the metaphor. It is linear. It is sequential. And each step is discrete and static. As seen with the Pulsar NX, this process proved inadequate for dealing with newly emerging ideas and shifting perspectives within the corporation. Any planning methodology resistant to acknowledging or reacting to these inevitable shifts is doomed to fail. And the only eventuality that can be counted on with any certainty in this scenario is target-shifting. Which means, when the bull's-eye is perceived as having altered its position, not only does "aim" become adjustable, but the very meaning of "ready" is transformed. In this more dynamic matrix, "ready" means not only a position fixed at the outset of an enterprise, but also a continuing capacity for remaining *in a state of readiness* for any eventuality.

None of this is to suggest that you are obliged to use planning for every novel thought or shift in the environment that arises during a project. Eventually, a line must be drawn, and even worthwhile ideas must be rejected or withheld for later application. Planning should take on a role of advocacy, one far more proactive and responsive to change than currently exists.

❊❊❊

When I caught sight of an envelope addressed to me from the office of Jerry Sanders, chief of the SDPD, I figured I'd had it. I did not know exactly what I had done, but I knew it had to be *something*.

Instead of a summons, however, the letter turned out to be an invitation from a Captain Leslie Lord to address the top brass of the San Diego Police Department on creativity and my experiences in shaping NDI. Captain Lord had heard a speech I had given to a group of community and business leaders called LEAD, and felt it would be interesting to the police force.

I have had the good fortune of addressing an incredibly diverse group of audiences all over the globe on the topics raised in this book. I have met and spoken about the subject with Crown Prince Naruhito of Japan, and the somewhat tarnished crown prince of America, W. J. Clinton, the struggling heads of immense corporations, and those of enterprising start-ups running on nothing more than the charge of a single idea and some venture capital. While I was relieved I had not been collared by the SDPD, none of these experiences prepared me for the apprehension I felt about addressing these issues with the Heat!

It was one thing to talk about abrasion, risk, and failure when what was at stake was a loss of ideas, market share, or profit—rather than life itself. But Captain Lord assured me that what I had to say was just what the officers needed.

Captain Lord told me that the SDPD, considered one of the country's most progressive and effective police forces, "had been undergoing a steady period of dramatic change to remain on the cutting edge of every major issue of law enforcement. Even though our worlds are very different," she continued, "when I heard you speak I realized we were dealing with similar issues: encouraging intuitive, on-the-spot thinking, dealing with risk and abrasion, learning from failure, handling the stress of change, keeping everyone fresh and stimulated and involved." Captain Lord had correctly intuited the connection between the resistance to creative thought and the threat of change, and felt NDI's experiences and outlook offered insights the SDPD needed.

Effective police work requires rote familiarity with well-learned procedures. The checklists and routines provide a considerable sense of security when dealing with complex, highly unpredictable and dangerous situations. But according to Captain Lord, the comfort in the routine had also spilled over into the way the department itself was managed. There was resistance to anything that wasn't familiar, so the issues being encouraged by Chief Sanders, such as the continual adaptation of new technologies or the creative use of community outreach programs, were generating considerable stress.

While I always like to tailor my talks to the group I am addressing, I am generally reluctant to apply the ideas to their specific issues, preferring to be surprised at how the people themselves employ them. And I certainly was not going to try to apply these strategies to a world as alien to me as police work. But I was terribly eager to understand just how they might hear and use what I had to say.

The department had taken a large, bare room at a bayside marina in the Mission Bay district of San Diego. The ocean breezes wafting in through the open windows from across the harbor seemed in perfect accord with the salty group of seasoned vets assembled there. Captain Lord had told me to expect some pretty direct communications and I was not disappointed, although I was surprised at the level of graciousness in the room. Cordial, polite cops (and anyone else whose uniforms include weapons) have always struck me as *especially* nice people.

The responsiveness and acuity of the questions and comments were as sharp as any I had experienced at the professional conferences or graduate schools I had addressed. And considerably more intimidating. Here was a group all too familiar with life-and-death situations, fascinated with such subjects as the constructive use of failure and the threat of creative thinking.

In the frenzy and fast-breaking turbulence of high-risk incidents involving armed individuals and many officers, one of the major perils is the inadvertent killing of police by other police. So the idea of *stepping back* from the situation while remaining in it to ask, "Now, what's going on here," seemed vitally interesting to them. It was clear that the procedures which were all-important to their success and salvation could be effectively augmented by synthesizing the intuitive dimensions of thought we had been discussing. And the need for near-instantaneous reactions in crisis circumstances would benefit from the ability to simultaneously consider possible adjustments to an *actual* "plan of attack."

Furthermore, here was the potential for a literal application of the more fluidly evolved notion of "ready, aim, fire" referred to earlier. The flexibility and mutual responsiveness of the "readying," "aiming," and "firing" turn out to be vital not only for effective planning and greater market share, but for remaining alive.

It was sobering to measure these ideas against the priorities of big-city police work. To my astonishment, they seemed to apply and to hold up. It was remarkable to me that the SDPD was interested in the topic at all; yet, asking for somebody from a field as remote as creative design to speak to police executives during a tough time of transition was a juxtaposition calling for about as extended a leap as Arthur Koestler ever dreamed of.

***

Business needs plans. Plans need ideas. Ergo, business needs ideas. Yet, currently prevailing ideas about plans tend to preclude ideas.

But once an organization has committed itself to the value of ideas and their essential role in idea-making, it has necessarily committed itself to dealing with a certain amount of surprise, disruption, and distress. These are easy words to write, but to many in the workplace they represent a very real threat.

Still, there are individuals like Keiichi Shinohara who, through his delight in the product, could energetically shift directions midway through a project yet remain "on track." Or Captain Leslie Lord, who could not only tolerate the intrusion of alien thinking but go out of her way to court it. Even at NDI, some are far more predisposed to unplanned change than others. And these are not necessarily people lacking in rigor, the need for accountability, or timeliness.

Mark Short is the exceptionally capable chief modeler of NDI's Blue Studio. He is also exceptionally goal-oriented, liking to receive and give clear direction and make steady progress. Yet, when a model on which he and his group have lavished countless hours of sensitive, skillful sculpturing is suddenly deemed off the mark, or a new idea appears to have greater potential, he can stop on a dime, reorient, and throw himself into the new direction with equal energy.

When I asked him how he was able to adapt to unexpected changes so easily, his response surprised me. "It's all about time for me. Time is my sport . . . it's why I swim." (Short is a powerful and graceful swimmer who does his laps religiously every noontime.) I asked him to explain further. "It's a question," he answered, "of how I use it, what I can do that's meaningful in an allotted period of time. If something interesting comes up, something that makes a significant and positive impact on the end product, then there's no question for me . . . it becomes a nonissue."

What Shinohara, Short, and Lord all have in common is a passionate concern for the quality of the end product, whether a functional concept like modularity, an expressive form like the fender of the Pathfinder, or the agility of a police department. The end goal is the continuing reference for their actions and reactions during a project. And the plan for them is a means to an end, a necessary and useful guide, but not an inviolable set of rules or sacrosanct dogma.

229

Because these three keep their eyes on the goal, the walls of the plan for them become transparent and porous to the continuing flux of the world beyond its bounds. While the defining limits of the plan can and should provide a filter to the surrounding environment, one that blocks nonrelevant or harmful elements but is open to the passage of potentially useful ingredients, it also allows for the exit of those aspects of the original strategy that no longer work or have become nonvalid.

Ironically, one of the great values of a well-conceived plan is the way it awakens a heightened sense of awareness of everything around us that might relate to it or prove useful in one way or another. Articles, books, television programs, and sites on the Net all dealing with the subject at hand seem suddenly to appear everywhere at once. Whenever I set out to do a painting, for example, I have a general notion of the direction I might like to take it. Once I begin, the world graciously provides me with a virtual smorgasbord of inspirational material from which to draw. Colors, patterns, relationships, and unfamiliar aspects of familiar objects all clamor for my attention. Of course, the world has not abruptly altered itself for my convenience. Instead, through immersion in a task with a clear overall direction, I have become reoriented and sensitized to potent aspects of my everyday experience that were always there but remained unseen. The world around me has not suddenly become new, but I can now see the world anew. Sadly, however, once a plan is in place, its walls are sealed and such serendipitous input is flatly rejected, even though it was stimulated by the plan itself.

By allowing the passage of such input, a plan becomes a porous, vital, breathing entity instead of a sealed container of rigid, increasingly stale preconceptions. And in so doing, it necessarily engages many of the strategies of the *creative priority* already discussed. Bringing together multiple disciplines for concerted action on emerging ideas would surely require the principles of *blurring the boundaries*. Once they were gathered in such high-pressure situations, *creative abrasion* would necessarily come into play, seeing the colliding concerns and perspectives as rich fodder for fresh thinking. And the very notion of reaching out to a planning department for leadership in accommodating and fostering potential change to its own plans would certainly constitute *embracing the dragon*, as would accepting that role from the viewpoint of the planners.

A *porous plan* is not a leaky vessel. Rather, it functions like the semipermeable membranes in all dynamic, living organisms, simultaneously containing and connecting the parts with the whole and the whole with the world.

***

It might at first seem odd to include something as potentially bureaucratic as the planning process in a book on creativity in business. In fact, there is an intimate relationship between planning and creativity. Since it is not possible to effect a plan without an idea, or an idea without a plan, they must be very much in sync with each other. When Pope Julius II decided his church needed some touching up and thought to invite Michelangelo to Rome to make some pictures for the ceiling of his Sistine Chapel, it was not only a good plan. It was one helluva good idea.

PART V

Conclusion

Welcome, O life! I go to encounter for the mil-
lionth time the reality of experience and to forge
in the smithy of my soul the uncreated con-
science of my race.

James Joyce[1]

12

Unending

I am reluctant to give this book any kind of tidy conclusion. The subject matter itself suggests a strong disposition toward a divergence of personalities and orientations, procedures and goals, precepts and concepts.

Several years ago, NDI convened a multidepartmental conference to help clarify and integrate the creative design activity in the largest possible corporate context. CEOs and key representatives came from Nissan affiliates all over America, Canada, and Mexico, as well as Japan. Presentations were made about the uses, abuses, and disuses of design from all perspectives, including those of Jay Chiat and Lee Clow from the corporation's adventurous ad agency, Chiat/Day. The core of the day was a frank and unusual roundtable discussion between key departmental leaders, led by Harvard law professor Charles Nesson, who had orchestrated many such "town meetings" for the eponymous PBS television series. Having seen how he skillfully elicited direct conversation on sensitive matters by concocting imaginary scenarios in which everyone played a part,

I felt he would be ideal in teasing out the cardinal issues concerning the problematic relationship between creative design and the organizational structure of Nissan.

By the end of the day, we had touched the surface of many of the issues that have been probed in these pages. While no concrete solutions were achieved, the overall awareness of both the difficulties and opportunities presented in dealing with creative work within large bureaucracies was significantly elevated. One-day conferences do not solve problems, but this one managed to identify and unravel many of them, leaving provocative loose ends lying all over the table.

Another of the outside consultants we had invited was Ralph Caplan, the prominent and highly articulate communications designer and writer on design from New York. He served as chief guru, roundtable participant, and keynote speaker. At the end of the long but fruitful day, we asked him to wrap things up. Instead, he delivered what he termed an "unwrapping" of the day's events, perceiving the very looseness of the ends we had exposed as the most valuable accomplishment of the proceedings.

Nothing deserves (or needs) an unwrapping more than the subject of creativity in organizations. No easy-to-digest executive summary is possible. The topic is, by definition, open-ended and ever-expanding, one confounding any attempt at all-inclusive summaries or final thoughts. I make no claims to have covered all possible strategies that might further the cause of ideation in business. Full chapters could easily be dedicated in some future book to such issues as the need for solitude, the importance of nuance, the opportunity for near-obsessive engagement in a project, and others not yet imagined.

The principles of the *creative priority* do not constitute a theory. They were not achieved through scholarship or the secondhand observation of subjects involved in a creative pursuit, as valuable as those approaches have been and will continue to be.

Rather, they represent a firsthand account of an ongoing enterprise, one that began by identifying idea-making as the centermost concern of a business. With that single act, the very meaning and business of our business was profoundly transformed in ways we could never have predicted. Revolutions begin not at the visible surface of a body of thought, but with deep shifts at its core. Although it would be presumptuous of me to posit these strategies as revolutionary, I can nonetheless report that their impact on *our* business and the people in it have been exactly that.

Many organizations have a moment or a period of innovative fluorescence. NDI has managed to sustain—or more accurately, continually invent—the means of stimulating and fostering a creative "moment" that has lasted for over eighteen years. Sales of NDI-designed vehicles (excluding general products) have passed the four-million-unit mark, and designs are already "in the can" for challenging new cars that will be introduced well into the next millennium.

The length of this creative span is highly unusual. It is rare even for exceptional groups such as the Xerox PARC (Palo Alto Research Center), which pioneered the personal computer; the Manhattan Project, that spectacular gathering of scientists at Los Alamos who created the atomic bomb; or Ital Design, the highly influential design studio of Turin, to maintain their creative sizzle for a period much beyond five to ten years. While some of these groups were assembled to deal with specific projects, businesses cannot afford to rely on brief or sporadic bursts of creative energy. Companies that have had great periods of innovative success at some point in their histories, such as General Motors, Apple, Motorola, Sony, and even the "imagineers" themselves, Disney, have felt the deadening threat of a waning of their creative powers. This book has delved into the principal ingredients of an ongoing creative momentum.

Still, this is not a system of thought, a prescription for "eleven steps to more and better ideas in business." None of the strategies covered can be applied out of the context of their original intent, or by themselves. As isolated procedures, they can have only temporary and limited impact. Over time, it has become clear to me that the creation of each one of them ultimately necessitated the creation of the others. For example, *hiring in divergent pairs* led to the necessity of treating individuals in various disciplines as aliens. The abrasion of *creative abrasion* ultimately softened and *blurred the boundaries* between disciplines. *Creative abrasion* also led to the coping mechanism of *embracing the dragon*, using oppositional positions as flint for creative sparks. And all of them led to a need for *well-informed intuitions* along with a highly *porous planning* process. They are inextricably linked to each other and the whole.

✳ ✳ ✳

While many corporations today are beginning to realize the increasing importance of sustained innovative ability as a competitive necessity, many will find it difficult to adopt the central proposition of this book. It is not that the changes effected by the new procedures are too complex or strange—in the deepest sense, they are nothing if not natural—but that they appear to threaten and run counter to familiar tactics for retaining control and avoiding risk.

Creativity has always been categorized as belonging to the "soft stuff," along with intuitive thinking, human resource management, motivational issues, employee assistance programs, and the like. The "tough stuff," all those aspects of business that can be nicely described by military and sports analogies, and justified by the assumed rigors of the hard sciences, retains a firm hold on most executive boards and graduate business school programs.

But it is interesting to compare the toughness quotient of the end products of a corporation with the traditional toughness of its management style. My experience has been that they are inversely proportional to each other. Those of us at NDI who came from one of the Big Three have found that our work has consistently been bolder and more advanced in San Diego than what we were doing in Detroit. Yet, while there, we were continually told to "go for it," to "scare the hell out of ourselves" with all-new forms and concepts. But all the cajoling, coercion, competition, and intimidation inevitably resulted in decisions and products that were cautious, reactive, and predictable.

What's wrong with that picture?

What's wrong is that tough thinking, decision-making, and management *really should* result in strong performance. But traditional toughness is in fact highly risk-averse, security-seeking, and uncertain in the face of the new. Dealing with the rigors of *informed intuition* and the hard arts of the creative process, on the other hand, turns out to require considerable gutsiness and the courage to genuinely engage with the new.

However, the kind of toughness required for leading the *creative priority* is quite different in quality than that associated with the traditional model. And a careful reading of the eleven strategies in this book will reveal many clues to new styles of management and leadership.

Struggling every day with these issues, it is sometimes difficult for us to recognize the profound shift that has occurred in the pervading atmosphere of our own company. Whenever visitors arrive at NDI, we are always surprised at how rapidly they "get it." The composite impact of everything—from the design of the logo to the architecture, from the products on display to what is visible but not "on display," and the way people are dressed and move and interact—is powerful, clear, and revealing. Such an ambiance cannot be faked or turned on for show. The energy, spontaneity, and passion for the work are all palpable. Perhaps most telling, NDI registers a particularly high smile quotient.

A high smile quotient had never been identified as a management goal. Nor were most of the other manifestations of the *creative priority*, with the exception of making a good place to create lots of ideas. But along with consistently high productivity, quality, and efficiency, all the aforementioned attributes seem to naturally accompany our commitment to an idea-fostering culture.

None of this is to say that NDI has achieved heaven on earth. Heaven help us if that were the case, as creative ferment is allegedly not a high priority there. Employees and their spouses and special others can all report that this way of working brings with it its own brand of anxiety and stress. The object was never to achieve perfection. Rather, it was to create a situation where it was safe to strive for it.

❊❊❊

It would be great to declare that this small satellite of Nissan has transformed the global character of the entire corporation. It has not, although it has certainly had a significant and growing influence. While our internal structure is as nearly an ideal situation as I can imagine in support of ideation, it would be misleading to say that the parent corporation and its worldwide network of subsidiaries has prioritized creativity. Still, the impact we have had has enabled us to see a far greater percentage of our ideas reach production in a pure form than I ever thought possible in a vast corporation. Furthermore, many of these strategies have found their way into the language and methodologies of other departments and other cultures.

But even if all the strategies suggested in this book were invoked and followed religiously, creativity would still sit uneasily within bureaucratic bounds. The chapter titles themselves indicate that its intrinsic nature is to unsettle, reorient, blur, engage demons, and abrade the status quo. None of the procedures is designed to make it a comfortable, obeisant, timely, well-oiled cog in traditional *or* enlightened bureaucratic machinery. Instead, the strategies were conceived to help overcome the knee-jerk resistance that inevitably accompanies the creative process, and to recognize the unease as a sign of its probable health.

In any traditional setting, it must be said that corporate policy will win out every time over idea-making. History is replete with examples of the way repressive, totalitarian governments have killed creative thought. And they are smart to do so, as divergent thinking does indeed represent the single most undermining threat to their continued power. This unique combination of fragility and power is a defining characteristic of creativity, one it shares with all living organisms.

Its power to undermine repression is the flip side of its even greater power to humanize. On every dimension, we have been gratified to find that what is supportive of original thought is supportive of people.

With imagination's need to engage and draw directly on life as its principal source of inspiration, the work/life boundary is necessarily blurred. The worker "unites himself with the world in the act of creation," said the psychologist/writer Erich Fromm.[1] Issues of daily existence are welcomed into the workplace not as intrusions but as germane material to be expressed and used. Rather than a community of labor isolated from the society outside the corporation, it becomes intimately connected with it.

I would certainly not claim that my principal reason for having prioritized the process of innovative thinking was its civilizing influence. I had something more pragmatic and urgent in my mind. What I really wanted was to work at a place that would get the hell out of my way so I could *think*. Having struggled to do my job under a system of management based on a profound misunderstanding of the way people actually use their minds, my paramount motivation was to structure an organization around a more realistic assessment of the intrinsic ways we are all wired. That seemed a pretty reasonable thing to do. The notion that a place of business might actually stimulate and enhance my thinking only grew as a real possibility over time.

***

Given the volatile nature of these concluding years of the twentieth century, it is not hard to understand why business has reinvented itself. New knowledge, new professions, new markets, and new technologies spawn new industries, which in turn spawn yet newer technologies, all spiraling outward in a vortex of increasing speed and complexity. Any business that resists change does so at its own peril, regardless of its size, history, or level of success.

All businesses need the rudder of an organizing principle to navigate through turbulent times. This is something deeper, more organic and useful than the traditional banality of most vision statements. The trick is to identify one broad enough, important enough, and central enough to propel and sustain coherence, change, and growth. Just as mathematics continually seeks the largest possible set to contain the greatest number of variables, so business searches for an organizational theme that can subsume and lend order to its dense and varied issues. While no single paradigm can work for every business, this book has asserted that the priorities of the creative process constitute a set with a scope of unexpected size.

Most organizations continue to believe that the issues of productivity, efficiency, or quality control are large enough to contain a business. These, however, are characteristics more associated with machines and hierarchical systems than with groups of human beings working together. People and ideas are less easily contained, far less predictable, and infinitely more complex. The *creative priority* begins with ideas and people and, as a set, easily contains the customary issues as well.

The full scope of the creative process has long lain buried, assigned low priority within the traditional preoccupations of business. While it has been thus confined, the only hint of its broad reach and imposing scale has been the sense of discomfort and threat it evokes and the prevailing need to constrain it.

Of course, there are many companies concerned with leading-edge concepts. They are capable of producing innovative products, inventive technologies, and original notions about service, distribution, or sales. Few of these, however, have grasped the full implications of their creative capabilities, restricting their application to what they make without seeing their significance to *how they do it* and *who they are*. The distinction between an innovative corporation and one with creativity at its core is what this book is about.

The *creative priority*, therefore, is not a concept to be limited to companies like NDI, which are specifically in the business of idea-making. Nor is it meant to be deployed only in creative departments. It is hard to imagine a business, an institution, or a department that could not be profoundly energized, liberated, and humanized by the recognition of the breeding of original thought as its preeminent organizing principle.

Imagine it.

***

Unend

Notes

Epigraph

1. T. S. Eliot, *Four Quartets/Little Gidding* (Harcourt, Brace & World, 1952), 145.

Introduction

1. Silvano Arieti, *The Magic Synthesis* (HarperCollins, 1976), 376–77.

Part 1

1. Neils Bohr, as quoted by Werner Heisenberg in *Physics and Beyond: Encounters and Conversations* (HarperCollins, 1971), 102.

Chapter 1

1. Arthur Koestler, *The Act of Creation* (Macmillan, 1965), 121.
2. *Design: Speed*, directed by Eila Hershon and Roberto Guerra (RM Associates, November 15, 1990).
3. Jeremy Bernstein, *Experiencing Science: Profiles in Discovery* (HarperCollins, 1980), 3.

Notes

Chapter 2

1. Electronic Data Systems

Chapter 3

1. Lewis Carroll, *Alice's Adventures in Wonderland* (Puffin Books, 1962), 26.

Part 2

1. Rollo May, *The Courage to Create* (W. W. Norton & Company, 1975), 14.
2. Charles Hartshorne as quoted by John Horgan in *The End of Science* (Addison-Wesley Longman, inc. 1966), 264.

Chapter 4

1. David Bohm, *Fire in the Crucible* (St. Martin's Press, 1988), 105.

Chapter 5

1. *The New York Times* (05, 03, 1989).
2. Robert Grudin, *The Grace of Great Things* (Houghton Mifflin, 1990), 53.

Chapter 6

1. *Cash Box* (September 25, 1959), 16.
2. Silvano Arieti, *The Magic Synthesis* (HarperCollins, 1976), 376–7.

Part 3

1. Robert Scott Root-Bernstein, *Discovering* (Harvard University Press, 1989), 265.

Part 4

1. Johann W. Goethe, *Elective Affinities* (Oxford University Press, 1994, 158.
2. Rollo May, *The Courage to Create* (W. W. Norton & Company, 1975, 14.

3. Jerome Bruner, *On Knowing: Essays for the Left Hand* (Harvard University Press, 1962), 18. By the President and Fellows of Harvard College.

Chapter 10

1. Theodore M. Porter, *Trust in Numbers: The Pursuit of Objectivity in Science and Public Life* (publisher, date), page number.
2. George Bernard Shaw, *The Portable Bernard Shaw* (Penguin Books, 1977), 604.
3. Don Gifford, *The Farther Shore: A Natural History of Perception* (Grove/Atlantic, 1990), 115.
4. Werner Heisenberg, *Physics and Beyond: Encounters and Conversations* (HarperCollins, 1971), 101.
5. Henri Poincaré, *Science and Method* (Dover Publications, 1952), 59.
6. S. Chandrasekhar, *Truth and Beauty* (University of Chicago Press, 1987), 66.

Chapter 11

1. Jerome Bruner, *On Knowing: Essays for the Left Hand* (Harvard University Press, 1962), 18. By the President and Fellows of Harvard College.

Part 5

1. James Joyce, *A Portrait of the Artist as a Young Man* (Viking Penguin, 1964), 253.

Chapter 12

1. Erich Fromm, *The Art of Loving* (HarperCollins, 1956), 17.

Selected Bibliography

Arieti, Silvano, **Creativity: The Magic Synthesis** (New York: Basic Books, Inc., 1976).

Arieti, Silvano, **The Intrapsychic Self: Feeling, Cognition, and Creativity in Health and Mental Illness** (New York: Basic Books, Inc., 1967).

Barrow, J.D., **Pi in the Sky: Counting, Thinking and Being** (Oxford: Oxford University Press, 1992).

Barzun, Jacques, **The Culture We Deserve** (Middletown: Wesleyan University Press, 1989).

Bateson, Gregory, **Mind and Matter: A Necessary Unity** (New York: Bantam Books, Inc., 1979).

Bernstein, Jeremy, **Science Observed: Essays out of My Mind** (New York: Basic Books, Inc., 1982).

Bernstein, Jeremy, **Experiencing Science: Profiles in Discovery** (New York: E. P. Dutton, 1978).

Birdwhistell, Ray L., **Kinesics and Context: Essays on Body Motion Communication** (Philadelphia: University of Pennsylvania Press, 1970).

Bohm, David, and F. David Peat, **Science, Order, and Creativity** (New York: Bantam Books, 1987).

Bramly, Serge, **Leonardo: Discovering the Life of Leonardo da Vinci** (New York: Harper Collins, 1991).

Bruner, Jerome, **On Knowing: Essays for the Left Hand** (Cambridge: Harvard University Press, 1962).

Campbell, Jeremy, **Grammatical Man: Information, Entropy, Language, and Life** (New York: Simon and Schuster, 1982).

Carroll, Lewis, **Alice's Adventures in Wonderland** (New York: Puffin Books, 1946).

Casey, Edward S. **Imagining: A Phenomenological Study** (Bloomington: Indiana University Press, 1976).

Chandrasekhar, S., **Truth and Beauty: Aesthetics and Motivations in Science** (Chicago and London: The University of Chicago Press, 1987)

Czikszentmihalyi, Mihaly, **Flow: The Psychology of Optimal Experience** (New York: Harper and Row, 1990).

Davis, Philip J., and David Park, ed., **No Way: The Nature of the Impossible** (New York: W. H. Freeman and Company, 1987).

Dunham, William, **Journey Through Genius: The Great Theorems of Mathematics** (New York: John Wiley and Sons, Inc., 1990).

Dyson, Freeman, **Disturbing the Universe** (New York: Harper and Row, 1979).

Eco, Umberto, **Travels in Hyper Reality** (San Diego: Harcourt Brace Jovanovich, 1986).

Ehrenwald, Jan, M.D., **Anatomy of Genius: Split Brains and Global Minds** (New York: Human Sciences Press, 1984).

Ehrenzweig, Anton, **The Hidden Order of Art: A Study in the Psychology of Artistic Imagination** (London: Weidenfeld and Nicolson, 1993).

Eiseley, Loren, **The Immense Journey** (New York: Vintage Books, 1959).

Eiseley, Loren, **The Firmament of Time** (New York: Atheneum, 1974).

Eiseley, Loren, **All the Strange Hours: The Excavation of a Life** (New York: Charles Scribner's Sons, 1975).

Eliot, T.S., **The Complete Poems and Plays: 1909-1950** (New York: Harcourt, Brace and World, 1952).

Eysenck, H. J., **Sense and Nonsense in Psychology** (Baltimore: Penguin Books, 1968).

Ferris, Timothy, **Coming of Age in the Milky Way** (New York: Anchor Books, Doubleday, 1988).

Feynman, Richard, **"Surely You're Joking, Mr. Feynman": Adventures of a Curious Character** (New York, London: W. W. Norton and Company).

Fromm, Erich, **The Art of Loving** (New York: Harper Colophon, 1962).

Gardner, Howard, **Frames of Mind: The Theory of Multiple Intelligences** (New York: Basic Books, 1983).

Gass, William, **On Being Blue: A Philosophical Inquiry** (Boston: Godine, 1991).

Ghiselin, Brewster, **The Creative Process: A Symposium** (New York: Mentor, 1952).

Gifford, Don, **The Farther Shore: A Natural History of Perception, 1798-1984** (New York: The Atlantic Monthly Press, 1990).

Gleick, James, **Genius: The Life and Science of Richard Feynman** (New York: Pantheon Books, 1992).

Goethe, J. V. von, **Elective Affinities** (Oxford, New York: Oxford University Press, 1994).

Goodrich, Lloyd, **Thomas Eakins** (Cambridge: Harvard University Press, 1982).

Gould, S. J., **Time's Arrow, Time's Cycle: Myth and Metaphor in the Discovery of Geological Time** (Cambridge: Cambridge University Press, 1987).

Grudin, Robert, **The Grace of Great Things: Creativity and Innovation** (New York: Ticknor and Fields, 1990).

Grudin, Robert, **Time and the Art of Living** (New York: Harper and Row, 1982).

Grudin, Robert, **On Dialogue: An Essay in Free Thought** (Boston, New York: Houghton Mifflin, 1996).

Hall, Edward T., **The Hidden Dimension** (New York: Anchor Press/Doubleday, 1969).

Hall, Edward T., **The Silent Language** (New York: Anchor Press/ Doubleday, 1973).

Hall, Edward T., **Beyond Culture** (New York: Anchor Press/Doubleday, 1977).

Hall, Edward T., **The Dance of Life: The Other Dimension of Time** (Garden City, New York: Anchor Press/Doubleday, 1983).

Heisenberg, Werner, **Physics and Beyond: Encounters and Conversations** (New York: HarperCollins, 1971).

Joyce, James, **A Portrait of the Artist as a Young Man** (New York: Viking, 1960).

Jung, C. G., **The Spirit in Man, Art, and Literature** (Princeton: Princeton University Press, 1966).

Kael, Pauline, **I Lost It at the Movies** (New York: Bantam Books, 1965).

Kanigel,Robert, **The Man Who Knew Infinity: A Life of the Genius Ramanujan** (New York: Charles Scribner's Sons, 1991).

Koestler, Arthur, **The Act of Creation** (New York: Dell, 1964).

Koestler, Arthur, **Janus: A Summing Up** (New York: Vintage Books, 1979).

Kohn, Alfie, **No Contest: The Case Against Competition** (Boston: Houghton Mifflin, 1986).

Kuhn, Thomas S., **The Structure of Scientific Revolution** (Chicago: The University of Chicago Press, 1970).

Langer, Susanne K., **Feeling and Form** (New York: Charles Scribner's Sons, 1953).

Langer, Susanne K., **Philosophy in a New Key: A Study in the Symbolism of Reason, Rite, and Art** (Cambridge: Harvard University Press, 1979).

Langer, Susanne K., **Problems of Art: Ten Philosophical Lectures** (New York: Charles Scribner's Sons, 1957).

Leshan, Lawrence, and Henry Margenau, **Einstein's Space and Van Gogh's Sky: Physical Reality and Beyond** (New York: Macmillan, 1982).

Maslow, A. H., **The Farther Reaches of Human Nature** (New York: Viking, 1971).

May, Rollo, **The Courage to Create** (New York: Bantam, 1976).

Miller, Arthur I., **Insights of Genius: Imagery and Creativity in Science and Art** (New York: Springer-Verlag, 1996).

Monk, Ray, **Ludwig Wittgenstein: The Duty of Genius** (New York: The Free Press, 1990).

Moore, Ruth, **Tale of a Danish Student; Neils Bohr: The Man, His Science, and the World They Changed** (Cambridge: M.I.T. Press, 1985).

Nozick, Robert, **Philosophical Explanations** (Cambridge: Harvard University Press, 1981).

Nozick, Robert, **The Examined Life: Philosophical Meditations** (New York: Simon and Schuster, 1989).

Poincaré, Henri, **Science and Method** (Bristol: Thoemmes Press, 1996).

Porter, Theodore M., **Trust in Numbers: The Pursuit of Objectivity in Science and Public Life** (Princeton: Princeton University Press, 1995).

Prigogine, I., and I. Stengers, **Order out of Chaos** (London: Heinemann, 1984).

Reischauer, Edwin O., **The Japanese** (Cambridge: Harvard University Press, 1978).

Rifkin, Jeremy, **Time Wars: The Primary Conflict in Human History** (New York: Henry Holt and Company, 1987).

Rivlin, Robert, and Karen Gravelle, **Deciphering the Senses: The Expanding World of Human Perception** (New York: Simon and Schuster, 1984).

Root-Bernstein, Robert Scott, **Discovering: Inventing and Solving Problems at the Frontiers of Scientific Knowledge** (Cambridge and London: Harvard University Press, 1989).

Snow, C. P., **The Two Cultures and a Second Look** (Cambridge: Cambridge University Press, 1969).

Sternberg, Robert J., **The Nature of Creativity: Contemporary Psychological Perspectives** (Cambridge: Cambridge University Press, 1988).

Stillinger, Jack, **Multiple Authorship and the Myth of Solitary Genius** (New York and Oxford: Oxford University Press, 1991).

Storr, Anthony, **The Dynamics of Creation** (New York: Ballantine Books, 1993).

Storr, Anthony, **Solitude: A Return to the Self** (New York: The Free Press, 1988).

Theroux, Alexander, **The Primary Colors: Three Essays** (New York: Henry Holt and Company, 1994).

Watson, James D. **The Double Helix: A Personal Account of the Discovery of DNA** (New York: Atheneum, 1968).

Weiner, Norbert, **Invention: The Care and Feeding of Ideas** (Cambridge: The M.I.T. Press, 1993).

Weiner, Norbert, **Ex-Prodigy: My Childhood and Youth** (Cambridge: The M.I.T. Press, 1964).

Weintraub, Stanley, ed., **The Portable Bernard Shaw** (New York: Penguin Books, 1977).

Wechsler, Lawrence, **Seeing Is Forgetting the Name of the Thing One Sees: A Life of Contemporary Artist Robert Irwin** (Berkeley and Los Angeles: University of California Press, 1982).

Whorf, Benjamin Lee, **Language, Thought, and Reality** (Cambridge: M.I.T. Press, 1964).

Whyte, William H., **City: Rediscovering the Center** (New York: Doubleday, 1988).

Wittgenstein, Ludwig, **Remarks on Color** (Berkeley and Los Angeles: University of California Press, 1977).

Zajonc, Arthur, **Catching the Light: The Entwined History of Light and Mind** (New York: Bantam Books, 1993).

Index

Index

Index

Index

259

Index

JERRY HIRSHBERG, a native of Cleveland, Ohio, left General Motors in 1980 and accepted the position of founding director of Nissan Design International, Inc. He speaks widely on subjects ranging from automotive and productive design to multicultural business to the managing of creative capabilities. An accomplished painter and musician, he lives and works in Del Mar, California, with his wife, Linda.